REMARKABLE READS

REMARKABLE READS

34 Writers and Their Adventures in Reading

Edited by J. PEDER ZANE

W. W. Norton & Company

New York London

Copyright © 2004 by J. Peder Zane

All rights reserved
Printed in the United States of America
First Edition

Manufacturing by the Haddon Craftsmen, Inc.
Book design by Blue Shoe Studio
Production manager: Amanda Morrison

Library of Congress Cataloging-in-Publication Data

Remarkable reads : 34 writers and their adventures in reading / edited by J. Peder Zane—1st ed.
        p. cm.
Essays which first appeared in the Raleigh News & Observer.
ISBN 0-393-32540-7 (pbk.)
 1. Authors, American—20th century--Books and reading. 2.
Authors—20th century—Books and reading. 3. Books and reading.
I. Zane, J. Peder.
 Z1039.A87 R46 2004
 028'.9--dc22
                                        2003021074
W. W. Norton & Company, Inc.
500 Fifth Avenue, New York, N.Y. 10110
www.wwnorton.com

W. W. Norton & Company Ltd.
Castle House, 75/76 Wells Street, London W1T 3QT

1 2 3 4 5 6 7 8 9 0

CONTENTS

INTRODUCTION

Adventures in Reading

It's literature's version of the chicken and the egg: Who makes books come alive, writers or readers?

Anatole France said a writer's words are "a magic finger that sets a fibre of the brain vibrating like a harp string" and "so invokes a note from the sounding board of the soul." But he also observed that it is the reader's response that makes those words "dull or brilliant, hot with passion or cold as ice."

Imaginative writers need sensitive readers just as surely as pianists need finely tuned instruments and just as surely as chickens need eggs—and eggs need chickens. The thirty-four essays in this book explore the symbiotic relationship between remarkable books and remarkable readers. They show us how books can tempt and enchant us—if we let them. They tell us why they can be dangerous, sad, lonely and mad, fragile and fearless, seductive and devastating, unpleasant, daunting and yes, sometimes, incomprehensible—if we're of a mind.

Can a book be Scottish, smokin' or double-d-daring? You tell me.

Each of the thirty-four authors describes a specific

encounter with a book, suggesting the varieties of literary experience. Together they draw on works from an array of writers including Eudora Welty, Richard Ford, Sigmund Freud, and Louis L'Amour. They explore classic texts such as *The Catcher in the Rye, Doctor Zhivago, Absalom, Absalom!, The Cat in the Hat,* and Hans Christian *Andersen's Fairy Tales.* And they plumb wonderful obscure works including *The War with the Newts* by Karel Čapek, *The Worm Ouroboros* by E. R. Eddison, *Sunset Song* by Lewis Grassic Gibbon, and *Stick and Rudder: An Explanation of the Art of Flying* by Wolfgang Langewiesche.

None of us at the *News & Observer* could have guessed the imaginative range the writers would bring to the series when I proposed the idea to my editors, Melanie Sill and Felicia Gressette. We began with a rough notion of where we wanted these adventures in reading to go—and the places to avoid. Have writers discuss their favorite books, but don't produce another series where writers . . . discuss their favorite books. Push them to describe the ineffable powers of literature . . . without resorting to highfalutin platitudes about the ineffable powers of literature. Discourage laundry lists of works they loved as children. Encourage specificity and detail. Above all, figure out a way to have great writers meet us at eye level, as readers.

With my altruistic friends, black coffee and nicotine gum, I hit upon the signpost that would lead these essays in the right direction: adjectives. We'd ask writers from around the country to pick a single book and a single adjective to describe their encounter with it.

At best we were hoping for neat twists on beloved works. What we received were deeply felt blends of literary criticism and the personal essay that read like short stories. Instead of simply describing their literary tastes, they drew on signature moments from their lives to detail how they had brought books to life and how that experience had shaped them.

Books propel writers to take bold action. Charles Frazier traveled twenty-five hundred miles by car, train, and thumb from his North Carolina home to northern Mexico's canyon country because he had to see for himself the "tempting" land of native Central Americans that Antonin Artaud reveals in *The Tarahumara*. Marianne Gingher risked her career and reputation to meet Eudora Welty because she was so emboldened by the great Mississippian's "double-d-daring" novel, *The Robber Bridegroom*.

Books struck other writers like lightning bolts. Elizabeth Hay found the cure for her deep blues in a collection of Pauline Kael's "fearless" movie reviews. Aimee Bender finally understood her mother's love for modern dance after immersing herself in the deeply "intuitive" prose of Haruki Murakami. And Lee Smith mustered the strength to start a novel after reading Katharine Butler Hathaway's "luminous" story of courage, *The Little Locksmith*.

One of the most refreshing results of these love's labors was the reminder that books can take hold of us anytime, anywhere. Thus these essays are arranged in a rough chronological order—beginning with encounters in youth, then on to books confronted in early adulthood, midlife, and later life.

As a young boy, Robert Morgan read the great Russian novel *Doctor Zhivago* at "odd moments between field work and homework, milking the cow and helping to make molasses." Boris Pasternak's "wise" work provided intimations of worlds outside his rural North Carolina community while also confirming for Morgan that his people and his places were the stuff of literature.

Peter Gay did not read Victor Klemperer's diaries of Nazi Germany until nearly a half century after he had fled Hitler's nightmare—an escape many of his family members did not make. Gay, a scholar of the period, found Klemperer's book was full of "surprises," reminding him that literature can always and forever help us see the world anew.

Do we read books or do books read us? It's an ancient riddle that Bret Lott solves with the answer: It depends on when we read them. He was an angry and alienated college student when he first opened *The Catcher in the Rye* and cheered Holden Caulfield's youthful assaults against the grown-up phonies. Lott was a forty-year-old parent rearing children beginning to navigate a treacherous world when he reread the work and found himself worried by the "fragile" hero's risky behavior.

As Lott suggests, it is impossible to arrive at a precise definition of literature because books can mean different things—often to the same person. The essays in this collection represent a multitude, a variety of voices and experiences, of sensibilities and opinions. And yet, these variegated adventures in readings all strive toward a common destination that offers the best definition I can imagine for literature—the quest for truth. "Emotional truth," Jill McCorkle writes, "that shining moment every writer is hoping to find."

Time and again, the writers describe the source of literature's power as its responsibility to reveal those hard and liberating insights that popular culture and personal fears compel us to avoid and deny. For Betty Adcock, Hans Christian Andersen's "enchanting" fairy tales suggest the "unusually powerful truth" that not every story—or life—ends "happily ever after."

Ben Marcus admired Richard Yates's "devastating" novel, *The Easter Parade*, because it reminds us "how temporary our lives are, how close to grief we constantly flirt. . . . We connect with a true reaction to the world that keeps us in mind of how deeply urgent it is to be alive."

And as Frederick Busch argues in his piece on William Saroyan's collection *The Daring Young Man on the Flying Trapeze and Other Stories*, good books are "dangerous" because they do not simply tell us the truth but challenge us to live up to their high ideals. Saroyan's advice, "Try to be alive, you will be dead soon enough," is wise. But it is just a string of words. Only readers can bring them to life by taking them to heart.

O lucky reader, the book you hold offers thirty-four examples of readers who have accepted that challenge, who have made books come alive. They remind us that opening a book is a necessary first step, but the story's final word is still just the beginning. Literature offers unimaginable adventures—but they are journeys that go only as far as each reader is willing to take them.

Where do you want to go?

REMARKABLE READS

BEBE MOORE CAMPBELL

The Most Memorable Book I Read
THE CAT IN THE HAT by Dr. Seuss

My upwardly mobile mother believed that education was the foundation necessary for achieving America's promise, and that the cornerstone of education was memorization. To that end, she made sure that I began the process of sealing information inside my brain even before I entered school. I remember a Saturday evening before our large Baptist church's Easter pageant. I was on stage in the church's basement, swishing and crinkling my crinoline skirt as I hopped from one foot to another, spouting the four lines I had memorized for my performance:

I'm a little daffodil
and I have come to say:

. . . .

Bebe Moore Campbell is the best-selling author of five novels including *Your Blues Ain't Like Mine*, *Brothers and Sisters*, *Singing in the Comeback Choir*, and *What You Owe Me*. She has also written a book for children about mental illness, *Sometimes My Mommy Gets Angry*. She lives in Los Angeles.

Jesus Christ has risen,
Happy Easter Day.

Later, as I outgrew the children's Sunday school class and passed on to the Baptist Young People's Union, I left behind the sweet short stanzas of kiddie "pieces." Every two months or so I committed to heart a poem by Langston Hughes or something by the universally beloved Paul Laurence Dunbar. These I recited at any number of the church talent programs designed to showcase the musical, vocal, and dramatic skills of its youth. I put my heart and soul into Dunbar's poems, mastering the folksy Southern dialect of the enslaved people who inspired them. Through the years my repertoire grew, as did my self-confidence when I recited.

Under my mother's relentless coaching, I not only learned poems by heart but also books of the Bible, several Psalms, including, of course, the Twenty-third, as well as any number of speeches I wrote to perform in her sorority's annual oratorical contest. In elementary school, I mastered the alphabet, the multiplication tables, the states and continents in record time—I had, after all, been well trained.

I memorized so many pieces for middle and high school English teachers: *The Highwayman*, *Hiawatha*, innumerable excerpts from Shakespeare. If the incentive was great enough, there was no end to what my mind could retain. To gain the approval of my handsome biology teacher, I learned to identify the leaves of nearly every tree in Philadelphia's Fairmount Park. So great was my adoration for Mr. Dickerson, that I became a veritable encyclopedia of the deciduous.

Nevertheless, in my teenage years I began opposing my mother's efforts to force me to memorize and perform.

"But why can't I just read it?" I asked her after I'd written yet another essay for her sorority's contest.

She shook her head in consternation. "Anyone can read," she replied. "Besides, suppose you lose your paper?"

She was a stern taskmaster. The daughter of a maid and an itinerant preacher, she had, through dint of sheer academic excellence and willpower, won a full scholarship to the University of Pennsylvania, back in the 1940s, when African-American students on that campus could be counted on one hand. That Ivy League degree, as well as the two master's she earned, propelled her from the ranks of the poor into the middle class. My campaign for mediocrity was doomed.

I got it. What was in my mind couldn't be taken from me. Couldn't be lost. To commit anything to memory is to make it as much a part of you as your skin and breath. It is an empowering act. My mother wanted me to be strong.

And self-reliant. When I was three years old, I got lost in New York City. While my mother and godmother were chatting, I wandered away and the next thing I knew I was being driven around by two cheerful and very resolute police officers. I knew my Philadelphia address: 2239 N. 16th Street. But that was far away. Fortunately, my godmother lived on 116th Street. The cops thought that I couldn't pronounce one hundred, and so they kept circling the area until they passed by two frantic women, who tearfully retrieved me. You never know.

My mother was right about the permanence of what is memorized but only up to a point. Middle age and memory don't mix well. My mind has lost some of its youthful elasticity. These days I sputter my way through most Hughes and Dunbar poems. I do recall that Genesis is the first book of the Bible and Revelation the last but for the rest I go to the table of contents. And it's been a long time since I approached a podium without notes. Still, there is something of my mother's training left in me yet. Even now, I tend to memorize lines that are meaningful to me. Sometimes I learn what is linguistically appealing, what dazzles my tongue. But the older I get, the more likely I am to forgo semantics that offer mere pyrotechnic display. More often, I remember what teaches me, what spurs me on, what is wise. When I finish a book, just saying aloud the line or two that have stuck with me allows me to relive the wonder of the story, to recall the precise magic that the author has evoked. The lines literally jump from the page into my mind. These words say, "Keep me; I'm yours."

The Cat in the Hat, Dr. Seuss's silly, imaginative yarn contains the most uplifting passage I've ever memorized. The coolest cat of all times climbed into my heart when I was in the third grade, and he still makes it beat faster. His rhyming nonsense has always made perfect sense and helped me establish my own literary standards, to wit: Does the book delight me? Do the words captivate me? Does the tale horrify me, make me feel dread, make me laugh? Does the story resonate? Do I want to share it? Do I walk away with something in my head, welded to my heart? Did it make me a wiser person?

Anyone who doesn't know Dr. Seuss's seminal story has been in a coma for a very long time, but here it is in a nutshell: a rainy day, Mom's away, two bored, restless children, a knock at the door, the strangest cat ever enters and the fun begins. This is a book that uses rhyming nonsense words to describe the fantastic high jinks of a catman whose idea of fun is balancing a goldfish on top of an umbrella, while turning a household topsy-turvy to the chagrin of two hapless children who are as fascinated by his antics as they are terrified that their mother will return to a mess. The story captivates young minds, helping them fall in love with reading. The illustrations capture the cat's zany charm, the children's confusion and the goldfish's fear, and they introduce the world to a couple of characters so weird and wired that they can only be named Thing One and Thing Two. But that's not why I call it wise, nor why I sent a copy of it to my forty-something cousin, who was grieving the loss of his mother. And it's not why I reread it when I need spiritual uplift. Page seven says:

I know it is wet
And the sun is not sunny.
But we can have
Lots of good fun that is funny!

Gray days, of course, come unbidden to every life. Whether it's the dreariness of a child's boredom or the torrential downpour of a nation riven by terror, there are moments, days, years even, when the sun just isn't sunny. Dr. Seuss reminds us that we can make the best of a bad situation by being open to the possibility of adventure and even joy. Choose fun, the cat says. Take a risk.

Dylan Thomas put it one way: "Rage against the dying of the light." Ntozake Shange put it another: "Whatever good there is, get it and feel good."

The lines from *The Cat in the Hat* are my personal standouts but I've committed the words of other authors to memory. When I met Sandra Cisneros, MacArthur Fellow, poet and short story writer, on the brisk night of her University of Southern California appearance, I shook her hand and said, "a house the color of bad weather," quoting from her mesmerizing short story collection, *The House on Mango Street*, which describes both the burden and the beauty of being Latino in America. Her words are lodged in my heart. Gracie Mae Still, the shrewd blues-singing character who sold her signature tune to a swivel-hipped rock and roller in Alice Walker's short story, "1955," was eminently quotable. "The trick is to live long enough to put your young bluffs to use," she mused. And if I ever run into Pete

Dexter I will tell him how I trembled reading the last line of his redemptive novel *The Paper Boy:* "There are no intact men."

Cisneros's words are evocative and so perfect that I can't let them go because of the economic perfection of their rhythm, because they so precisely describe class and mood, and place each story so well in its own world. The line inspires and teaches. When I struggle for clarity, for what is concise and beautiful, these words are the standard. And Walker and Dexter deliver wisdom, so pure and unadorned, that it is cause for celebration.

Knowing an address is a practical use of memorization. The words I memorize from books serve a different purpose. Learning page seven of *The Cat in the Hat* doesn't improve my life in any functional way but the wisdom in those words lifts my soul and enables me to function. The Lord's Prayer, the Twenty-third Psalm, the Serenity Prayer, are touchstones for my existence as both a human and a spiritual being. Saying those words connects me to a source of unseen power that comforts and protects me. When I need that comfort, that protection, I don't want to have to go searching for it in a book. I want at least that part of the book to be in me.

To say something, over and over, mess up then repeat it again and again, teaches patience and standards. The reward, in addition to knowing the poem, the quote, the alphabet by heart is an appreciation for one's own power of concentration and willpower. And others appreciate it, too. This is why the church elders say amen after each recitation of an Easter piece. Amen! If you can stand before us and let the words flow from your mind, there's no telling what you can accomplish.

Not long ago, I accompanied my son-in-law to preschools he was considering for my eighteen-month-old granddaughter when she becomes three. The first school was a child's garden of creativity. There were guinea pigs and rabbits in cages on the playground.

There were plots where flowers and vegetables grew. The classrooms were bright and cheerful with colorful mobiles hanging from the ceiling. "What will she learn?" I asked the teacher eagerly.

"We don't push them," she replied. "We let them do what interests them."

"What about the alphabet, numbers, colors?" I asked.

"If that's what the child is interested in."

My son-in-law is from an immigrant family, as results-oriented as my mother's up-from-the-South clan of bootstrappers. Our eyes met for a moment; our eyebrows rose in unison.

The next school was run by its eighty-year-old founder, a small, dark-skinned woman with the energy of a twenty-year-old. The classrooms were clean but no fairytale wonderland by any stretch of the imagination. Outside, the children were playing noisily in the sandbox and at the water table. She concluded her well-organized orientation by saying, "By the time your child leaves here, she will know how to count to five hundred in fifteen minutes."

When I looked at my son-in-law, he was smiling, too.

JONATHAN LETHEM

The Loneliest Book I Read

THE HAPPY VALLEY by Eric Berne

I'm writing today about the loneliest book I've read—lonely in the wonderful sense that I've still never met anyone else who's read it. This has increasingly seemed a wonderful thing to me. I've learned to value, actually to crave, that old privacy that used to be my constant familiar when I read, whether I was still selecting children's books or making my earliest explorations of the grown-up's shelves. Books weren't surrounded, for me then, by reviews, awards, consensus, zeitgeist, or buzz. I never felt guilty for being the last to discover something, never felt smug or self-improving for reading something difficult. Instead, it was forever only me and a book on a lonely exploration. Me in a secret garden. And my loneliest book really was a secret garden—a children's book called *The Happy*

....

Jonathan Lethem has published five novels, including *As She Climbed Across the Table* and *Girl in Landscape*. In 1999, he won the National Book Critics Circle Award for Fiction for his novel *Motherless Brooklyn*.

Valley, it concerned an isolated land where people were permanently happy and strange. No one but me has ever broken in there, to *The Happy Valley*, so far as I know. The irony, though, is that my lonely book was written by one of the most famous authors in the world, at least at the time he wrote it.

His name was Eric Berne and if you were around in 1963 you probably read his famous book *Games People Play*, which held a spot on *New York Times* bestsellers lists for more than two years. Berne was among the fathers of something called Transactional Analysis, and in *Games* he became its popular explicator as well, and some kind of cultural star. This was that same moment when the Beatles dawned, and with them the "real" sixties; our parents were ready for a fully credentialed, fully bespectacled psychiatrist to explain hostilities and neuroses as "bad games" that could be identified and banished. The book is lucid and clever, with an air of existential empowerment, an antiauthoritarian tinge: institutions played bad games, whether they were governments, colleges, or families, relationships, or one's own hidebound mind. Autonomy was the higher sport. If you'd found yourself backsliding into a round of "Frigid Woman" or "Courtroom" or "Now I've Got You, You Son of a Bitch," well, it was only a game: start over. Berne's genius title found its meme-like way into the culture, giving title and lyric to both a country song by Joe South and a soul number by The Spinners—and that's how it's likeliest to be remembered now.

Then, as now, a pop guru with a two-year bestseller could rely on having his ephemeral jottings published, even if only as a courtesy—if Deepak Chopra has a children's book in him, you can bet his publisher will put it in hardcovers. Eric *Games People Play* Berne did have a children's book in him, *The Happy Valley*. Grove Press published it in 1968, some adult purchased it, removed the jacket (and thereby any evidence of its connection to *Games*) and gave it to me—I have the evidence here in my hands.

I've never had confirmation of the book's existence besides the copy in my hands. Unlike Bosco, The Bugaloos, Quisp and Quake, *Free to Be You and Me*, and other touchstones of my child-cultural experience that have not only been confirmed, but burnished into kitsch talismans, no one I've mentioned it to has ever heard of, let alone read, *The Happy Valley*. The book might as well have been scooped from an alternate world. Like any book in the mind of a child, it had the authority of its existence, which was all it needed then. My friends had *Alice's Adventures in Wonderland*, *The Phantom Tollbooth*, *The Lion, the Witch and the Wardrobe*, and *A Wrinkle in Time*: I had all of those and *The Happy Valley*, too. For me it was just as deep as those books, equally as a singular and self-contained fantasy. And unlike the others, it has never been decanted into adult context—no erotic photography or disguised Benjamin Disraeli, no Christian allegory, no disappointing movie adaptations. In my early twenties I worked in a bookstore that specialized in Oz books and Oziana. There my glimpses of the nerdish frenzy of the collectors, and the show-offy one-upmanship of the scholarly types, who sonorously graded the deficiencies of the commissioned sequels by Ruth Plumly Thomson, forever ruptured the magic bubble of the first book. This can never happen to *The Happy Valley*. *The Happy Valley* is mine, and it is safe.

The book isn't nearly as innocuous—okay, insipid—as its title. It's thrillingly weird. The protagonist is a blue python named Shardlu, who is introduced as "not very handsome to look at, and not very clever . . . the only way he could earn a living was by being kind to people on Tuesday night and Friday morning. He was listed on the payroll as "Friend & Companion." Shardlu has a bad dream that causes him to curl into a ball and roll downhill, where he bumps into a sign, which sets the unpretentious, unforced surrealist tone for the book:

You are now entering the valley of Lamador. Everybody will see something different here. You will see one thing and your father and mother and dog will see something else. A father will see big trees, big birds, and big animals. A mother will see little flowers, little birds, and butterflies. A dog will see little animals, big and little trees, and bones, but he will smell more than he will see. But the main thing that you will see is to see what happens next.

What does happen next has the deliriously digressive quality of a sunlit dream, or possibly four or five dreams drifting together like clouds. It involves Shardlu's engagement with the citizens of Lamador—a caravan of dressed, talking animals that include a rabbit named Dulcy and a sheep named Flossie. The animals are led by a strange idiot-sage elder with a long white beard, named Abe, who never answers questions, but often volunteers wisdom impromptu, such as his speculation that Shardlu has come to them from Australia: "I knew that the Australians were going to fall off sometime, and now it has happened . . . any fool can see that the Australians are hanging head downward." Also drifting through are an elegant Prince and a Princess with the air of spoiled, distracted lovers, not quite concerned with the main plot, and an explorer named "The Restless Nogo," who confesses he discovered Lamador the first time he ever left his house. A temperate crisis is caused by Shardlu's hunger, which he directs at Dulcy the rabbit—Shardlu recalls that his mother advised him to "always keep a little bunny for a rainy day." In this he falls into alliance with the Princess, who's been eyeing Dulcy's pelt for a rabbit-skin umbrella to protect the fragile jelly-bean house she's built to honor the Prince.

A vein of amoral generosity runs deep in Lamador—the creatures work diligently on a guilt trip good enough to persuade Dulcy to sacrifice herself to the python's hunger and the rabbit-skin umbrella, which, as the princess points out to the prince, "I promised you, and what's more important, I promised my conscience too." This wouldn't be 1968, though, if all apparently societal problems weren't in fact solvable in the realm of personal transformation. Handily, Shardlu has begun to itch, warning him that he may be ready for a major shedding. Everyone helpfully tugs at Shardlu's outer skin together, while he clamps his teeth around a tree—but the unforeseen effect is that the python flips inside out. He turns a bright pink color, and loses his reason and eyesight as well, and so gives blind, ravenous chase to Tobedwego, mistaking the lead robber for a meal. When Tobedwego escapes, Shardlu blissfully swallows himself, and vanishes.

Any time I've shown *The Happy Valley* to people familiar with children's books, they have the same quick response: that there's way too much text on the pages for a colorfully illustrated picture book, which is what it resembles in every other way. This may have dictated the book's failure in its day (I don't know this for a fact), but it isn't fair. I try not to get defensive—after all, anyone who resists is only confirming more deeply my private relationship to the book, the sense in which it is a dream recounted that only I'll ever completely understand. And the people I've handed the book to aren't children, so they can never approach it with the same receptiveness I did. And not everyone resists.

If you sit and read the book on its own terms the proportion of incident to illustration is, I think, quite reasonable. And what fills the pages, after all, are the lovely paradoxical dialogues:

"Do you know why you have to face front in an elevator?"
"No," said Dulcy.

*"Neither do I," said Abe. "So I always face the rear. It makes everyone
nervous as a cat."*

"Cats are nervous," said Flossie. "He's right, as usual."

These invariably enchant anyone I've managed to induce to dip
into them.

A mention of the illustrations, which are by Sylvie Selig. The
bright-hued pages are certainly characteristic of their era, for a certain
paisley-decorative splendor, and for the bell-bottoms and Nehru col-
lars on the animals' two-piece suits. The style, though, is mysterious
and wonderful and slightly naive, less Peter Max–slick than a sort of
cross between Henri Rousseau's paintings and Klaus Voorman's
jacket art for the Beatles' *Revolver*. And the drawings play a nice trick
I've never much seen elsewhere, one which made the book particularly spellbinding and rereadable for me as a child: they contradict
and amplify and even sometimes seem to mock the text itself. For
instance, where Shardlu's work as "Friend & Companion" is
described, the story also mentions his schedule of "breakfast on
Monday morning, lunch on Wednesday at noon, and dinner on Friday
evening." Nothing more, but Selig has depicted Shardlu grinning over
a plate of live—shrew? vole? Hard to tell—which pleads for its life.
This nicely sends up "Friend & Companion" as well as prefiguring the
rabbit-eating plot. Extra animals, unmentioned in the tale, clutter the
peripheries—pigs, monkeys, alligators, even lobsters and giant beetles
are shown joining in the communal hubbub. And as wordy as the
book is, it stops several times for silent pages, where Selig's lush, mysterious art bleeds to every margin. This has the effect of stopping
time. When I pick up *The Happy Valley*, which is often, I'm frequently
going back to gaze deeper into the odd depths of the drawings, rather
than rereading the tale from beginning to end.

But what about that plot? It needs finishing. Though he never quite "tuned in," Shardlu has, of course, dropped out and turned on quite heroically. His transformation doubly spares Dulcy's life, since the blue skin he shed before swallowing himself makes the Princess a fine umbrella. The Restless Nogo might have to wander on to find things to discover, until he is offered, by Abe, this insight: why not discover himself?

Finally, a happy banquet is laid out for all the creatures, including the suddenly returning Shardlu, who explains:

"I changed my mind. So I unswallowed myself backward so I would be right side out again, and here I am."

"Oh, my!" said Dulcy.

"Don't worry," said Shardlu. "I discovered that if you once swallow yourself, you can never be the same afterward. I don't want to eat Dulcy anymore. Now all I want are flowers and toys and hardware and jelly beans, and there are plenty of those things around."

"How did you change your mind?" asked the Princess.

Shardlu doesn't know how to answer, but Abe does, and it is here Berne tips his hat just slightly to his great model, Lewis Carroll: "You either swallow yourself or get to the other side of a mirror. I was there myself when I was younger."

So, there's the gift *The Happy Valley* brought me—it took me as far on the other side of the mirror as the Carroll books, its Hippie aura no less poignant and affecting than the Victorianisms of Alice. Here's the odd gift it brings me now: since *The Happy Valley* is entirely mine, it can still take me there, a little. I can still visit Lamador and have my bad vibes smoothed out by the happy inhabitants, the ever-so-slightly sexy sheep and rabbits, the droll Zen

Koan-ish wisdom of Abe, which in truth stands for the naive Utopian yearning of our parents' sweetest, most hopeful selves. Unlike The Restless Nogo, they may not have convinced me (or the world) to stay back there in the late sixties. But like Shardlu, I can roll in for a visit.

BETTY ADCOCK

The Most Enchanting Book I Read
ANDERSEN'S FAIRY TALES

The green cloth cover of this antique collection of Hans Christian Andersen's fairy stories is ragged at the corners, and faded so that the lines of the weave stand out. A paper illustration was once attached to the front, but all that remains of it is the corner of the Emperor's golden robe and one of his shoes with its upturned toe. This is the ruler who loved first the small brown bird, the real nightingale, then turned instead, with the fickleness of power, to an engineered thing, an artificial bird aglitter with jewels and able to sing only one mechanical waltz. We are still learning that story, and perhaps one day we will understand it.

The story of another Emperor, whose vanity caused him to walk naked and unknowing until a child spoke the truth about

. . . .

Betty Adcock is author of five books of poems, including *Intervale: New and Selected Poems*, which was cowinner of the 2003 Poets' Prize. Recipient of a Guggenheim fellowship, she is writer in residence at Meredith College in Raleigh, North Carolina, and a member of the faculty of the Warren Wilson MFA Program for Writers.

"The Emperor's New Clothes," came also from Andersen's pen, and surely that metaphor is reenacted every election year in this media-saturated culture.

Meanwhile, here is the hem of the Emperor's robe and his royal foot, all that is left of the paper picture. The book's green cover is stained with what might be strawberry jam or cherry soda or that red sweet stuff that used to come in miniature bottles made of wax. For all its wear, the spine of the book still carries a shining gilded title: *Andersen's Fairy Tales*—Illustrated by Arthur Szyk.

Inside the front cover is an inscription in my Aunt Mary's hand. She was the one who wore fine perfume as well as an air of the exotic from having lived in Mexico. She always brought interesting presents. This book was her gift to me in April 1946. I was seven years old. The pages have softened with use, and the book falls open at the slightest slant. The full-page illustrations, many in full color, keep their odd intensity, something terribly old in them. I feel now the identical tremor as in childhood, when I used to open this book the way one enters a dream, with joy and fear together. The gorgeous endpapers are a medley of figures in deep royal reds and purples, shiny gold and the green of dark velvet. Here proportion is forgotten, as the seated Emperor is as tall as the turreted castle, and a duck is as big as a boy. An enormous Snow Queen towers over.these double pages of toys and big-eyed, sad children. The tiny girl is perched on a daisy in the bottom corner. The steadfast tin soldier stands on his one leg. An angel bearing a child flies past, and St. Nicholas is driving by with strangely clumsy-footed reindeer. Just behind this panorama, the Marsh King rises threateningly, a malevolent dark brown root with green eyes and a golden crown on its almost-head. On one high rootlet a beautiful bird is singing. Just below, a small winged demon is falling. This brilliant chaos of illustrations, each dragging a kite's tail of associations in my memory, is almost a shock. I haven't opened this box of wonders for many years.

I don't remember the first time I read the stories. They seem to have been present in my childhood the way I was present in the small isolated farming town in East Texas where I grew up, just there, like the birds of the air, the musty plush parlor furniture in my grandmother's house, or the backyard fish pond that held not only fish and weeds and mosquitoes, but also a perfect piece of sky (in the right light), clouds and all.

Our little town had no library or bookstore. In place of a school library, there was one bookcase at the back of each classroom. It was a poor town in a poor region where nothing much happened except life: animals, our farm, acres of woods, creeks, lightning bugs in summer, hog killings in fall—and at school, fear and trembling at math speed-tests, terror at recess, the teasing because I couldn't run well, or climb, or do any of the things that mattered among bunches of kids on a school ground. I often missed much of the school year because of severe asthma.

A lonesome, only child, I became a wanderer in the woods and gardens at my grandmother's place, a prowler of barns, friend to the chickens and the farm goat. And I became a reader. I was lucky enough to have very old novels and books of poetry at my grandmother's, Book-of-the-Month Club selections at home, and comic books and mysteries from the drugstore. I had favorite reading spots. A wisteria vine that had been trained into a kind of round tree was one of these. Underneath was a private world, cool shade in broiling Texas summers, a little scented room stained with purple light in spring. I read in my grandmother's heavy porch swing, in the backseat of the car, on the stairs, anyplace would do, it didn't

even have to be quiet. I read everything, my aunt's ladies' magazines, my grandmother's *National Geographic*s and *Progressive
Farmer*s, the Bible, even schoolbooks. But during the time between
my seventh and eleventh years—I'm guessing here but it seems
about that—I read these fairy tales again and again.

I adored them all, but I had favorites. "The Garden of Paradise"
was one. In this tale a prince finds himself in an enormous cave
where the mother of the four winds, a fierce Icelandic-looking
woman, is roasting a whole stag. One by one her blustery sons
come home, each with an account of his travels . . . the West Wind
first, telling of "the forest wildernesses where the thorny creepers
make a fence between the trees, where the water snake lies in the
wet grass, and human beings seem to be superfluous." The South
Wind speaks of Africa, its savannahs with grass "green as an olive"
and the desert with its yellow sand that looks like the bottom of the
sea. The East Wind arrives from China, where he's been "dancing
around the porcelain tower till all the bells jingled." The prince travels with the East Wind to Paradise, where they will deliver a gift.
Paradise has (of course) a palace, and a fairy princess in the palace.
The wind will bring her a leaf the Phoenix inscribed with his beak
just before going up in flames, leaving his egg in the ashes to hatch
the future. The palace in Paradise has "walls the color of the bright-
est tulips in sunlight, and its ceiling is one enormous flower. . . . "
Looking out through a window in this wondrous structure, the prince
sees Adam and Eve, the Tree of Knowledge, and the Serpent.
"Weren't they thrown out?" he asks, and learns that "Time burned a
picture in each of the magical windows. These pictures were alive,
the leaves waved and people came and went like reflections in a
mirror. . . . All that had ever happened in the world lived and moved
on those windowpanes. Only Time could print such wonderful pictures." I loved the fabulous descriptions. Even the story's ending,

when the prince, too, fails Paradise and is cast out, seemed completely right.

Most of Andersen's stories have sad endings, and that may have been one of their attractions for me. At seven, I had already seen my mother vanish, her sudden death the new defining point in my life. I had lost a place as well, having been moved to another house, I had seen my father fold into himself, quit his job, become a wanderer in the forests, a hunter spellbound by grief, his tamped spirit somehow comforted by the rough riverbanks, the difficult chases, the dogs' companionship. Death and transformation were two things I understood. I think I knew instinctively that the tales in my favorite book held an unusually powerful truth in the absence of the usual "happily ever after."

That knowledge stays. It has influenced my poems, which readers have sometimes seen as dark. Around 1980, I attempted a long poem for the first time. It was, as many poems are, autobiographical. But the shape of the poem would be, I hoped, more than that. I based the poem on "The Wild Swans." In that story, eleven brothers are turned into swans by their wicked stepmother. They are swans by day but at nightfall become human, until first light feathers them again with bewitchment. Many things happen, as always in good stories, but most important is their sister's difficult task, for only she can break the spell by gathering and weaving stinging nettles into shirts, speaking no word until the shirts are done. She undertakes this painful project, and because of her odd occupation and her silence, is thought by townspeople to be a witch. Condemned to be burnt, she is still working on the last shirt as she is being driven in a cart to the burning place. The brothers fly beside her on their white wings, and land on the side of the cart, and one by one she throws the stinging shirts over them. "But the youngest was left with a swan's wing instead of an arm, for one sleeve was wanting in the shirt of mail." This was the fascinating part, when I was a child, and also when writing the long poem all those years later. Imagine . . . a swan's wing instead of an arm! Useless for any sort of practical work, and useless for flight, too. It was an incomplete disenchantment. And what else does any poet live under but just such a partial and interrupted spell? I used the framework of the fairy tale as metaphor for the places and events of my childhood, and for the interior life of the child I was. It was incidental but helpful to learn that the swan's flight-feathers made the best quill pens. Oh, yes, I believe in magic. It is how poems get made.

Theories about fairy tales come and go, and have not much interested me. Since I read the tales when I was young enough to know the difference between believing a story and knowing the facts, I also knew how to recognize the points where those differences became irrelevant. I don't know what current opinion holds about fairy stories. Are they cathartic? Educational? Do they allow the child's angers and frustrations to be projected onto harmless figures made of words? Is the death in Andersen's stories too much for children? Are the angels here not sweet enough? Is the language too beautiful, especially when describing great fear, fierce punishment, irretrievable loss, or unplanned transport? Is there too much heaven as well as too much hell?

"The Snow Queen" is one of the harshest and most beautiful of stories. It begins with a mirror invented by demons, a mirror that makes every good thing reflected in it shrink away to almost nothing, whereas every ugly and evil thing stands out and looks its worst. The demons run all over the world with it, so that there is no country that has not been shown itself in this mirror. When they try to fly to heaven with it, they drop the mirror and it shatters into fragments, into grains, each one with the power to distort. A sliver of this mirror in the eye changes everything, and a sliver in the heart turns it to ice. Do we not have just such a mirror of the world pressed on us from every side? Isn't there a sliver of distortion in every eye? A bit of ice in the heart?

I know it never hurt me to read these often brilliant satires, these near-allegories, these fantast's delicacies, these celebrations. Replete with overly harsh morals, the stories rise beyond these into art because they are beautiful in their darkness. In Andersen's world, all things live and possess a spirit. Even a broken-off piece of a bottle speaks its story in "The Bottle Neck." "The Old Street Lamp" details the adventures of an articulate street lamp about to be retired and melted down into something else. There are philosophical and musical flowers, a tin soldier in love, and many other animations. In "The Bell," the people search and search for the lovely bell whose sound they hear every day, and they find at last the tolling sea, into which a glorious sunset is falling. Everything that exists has a singing voice, a ringing, a speech, a spell, a story.

As a child, I could walk around farm and house and woods, and see there many of the very things in the stories. Andersen often wrote hymns of praise to nature, to common things, to simple tools and simple people. Could I not find these things as lovely in the real world, now that I had seen such praise?

Only in the long poem "The Swan Story," loosely based on Andersen's "The Wild Swans," have I written directly from anything in this book. But poets often use fairy tales. Since I last read "The Nightingale" in this book, I have read Keats's "Ode to a Nightingale." Since I read these fantastic journeys, I have read Chaucer and Shakespeare. Since I read these charming transformations, I have read Christopher Smart. Since I read these frightening descents into nightmare, I have read T. S. Eliot.

I know that I, like everyone in our country, must look at the world every day in the distorting mirror of the television and the computer screen. Yet I go on writing lyric poems and story poems, some sad, some celebratory. I do this for any number of reasons, but one of them is the notion of flying, of seeing, of finding the country of the imagination that does not distort the world but locates its mystery. It is that old incomplete disenchantment.

DENISE GESS

The Most Important Book I Read
THE STRANGER by Albert Camus

Why was a twelve-year-old girl reading Camus instead of Nancy Drew? Well, I'd read all the Nancy Drews, then moved on to the Dana Sisters and finally, tired of girl detective duos, moved on to the Hardy Boys. Afterward, unsatisfied, I was looking for something grown-up, a story that had nothing to do with kids—not even pairs of smart, fearless kids. I was searching for a book that would transport me to another world because my personal world seemed to be collapsing. I was hunting for a character in a different sort of trouble—emotional trouble.

At the time, my maternal grandmother was staying at our house; more accurately, she occupied the other twin bed against the wall in my room and she was dying—although no

Denise Gess is an essayist and fiction writer who lives in Philadelphia. She has published two novels, *Good Deeds* and *Red Whiskey Blues,* and a nonfiction book about the deadliest fire in American history, *Firestorm at Peshtigo*.

one would admit it. She had colon cancer and had undergone a colostomy, yet my parents and my grandfather and the teams of relatives who made weekly pilgrimages to our house for a year of Sundays to visit her believed there would be a miracle. I wanted a miracle, too. As part of an extended Catholic Italian-American family, I'd been raised on miracles and enormous leaps of faith in the face of illness or sorrow. But even that faith couldn't stifle the sound of my grandmother's discomfort or her painful moans breaking through the darkness each night in the bedroom we shared. One afternoon, after a visiting nurse had come to give her a B-12 shot and I helped her get back into bed, she waved her hand at me, pawing the air between us. I thought she was gesturing that she could do it herself and didn't need or want my help, but as she lay back against the pillow she looked at me, her gray eyes nearly drained of color and whispered, "Oh, Denny. I want to die."

"No you don't," I told her. Then as I pulled the sheet up, I heard myself revising, "No," I said. "You can't."

Two days later, I stole *The Stranger* from the library.

Our small south Jersey town was flat and unglamorous, a maze of looping, winding streets and courts of split-levels and ranches, mostly working class but working class with ambition, refugees from city life who saw the suburbs as a step up to sophistication. The public library was housed in the first floor of the old, defunct elementary school—a tall, boxy, maroon-brick building that sat alone on a rise just beyond the railroad tracks that coursed through town. Back then, the librarians were watchful, censoring young eyes and imaginations from the "adult" section where Madame Bovary and Emma and Anna Karenina lived, and of course, "Mur-salt," *The Stranger*. The title alone intoxicated me. With everyone at home in a state of anticipation mixed with false cheer, I was beginning to feel like a stranger to myself: urgent, wormy inside, uncertain. And wasn't there a stranger in my own room, a ghost of the woman I had thought invincible?

That day, I had my tartan plaid book bag with me, had looped it onto the handlebar of my bike. Once inside the library I became as stealthy as Nancy Drew (those mysteries had taught me something) until the moment I sensed it was safe to slip *The Stranger* into my bag. Careful not to raise any suspicion, I checked out an acceptable book, *The Adventures of Tom Sawyer,* and left the library.

I rode home faster than I thought possible, my sneakered feet slipping off the pedals, my legs rubbery with fear. I had become a criminal. I had broken one of the Ten Commandments; this was no venial sin. I was in mortal sin territory. I'd stolen with full knowledge and intent. If a car hit me and hurtled me into the air to certain death before I reached home, I was going straight to Hell unless I could find the wherewithal to murmur an "I'm sorry" before my body crashed, broken, to the ground. Still, it hardly mattered. I had the book I needed.

How telling that I took it to the basement, descending to the underworld of the house to read it. I can still hear the initial soft crack, feel the pop of air that accompanies the opening of any book. "Mother died today. Or, maybe, yesterday; I can't be sure." I reread those opening words at least a dozen times. I read them out loud, hearing both the strangeness and the utter beauty of a voice so detached from a mother's death.

Who was this speaker? I discovered Mersault was a man who not only seemed incapable of expressing the expected grief over his mother but who would, in the course of the story, commit a senseless murder, egged on by the blinding Algerian sun. When I finished the book, perplexed yet filled with love and hatred for Mersault, I knew somewhere inside my bones that this was what I wanted to be: a writer, but not just any writer. I wanted to be a bold writer who would surprise and seduce by the sheer directness and unsavoriness of her words.

Mersault spoke of a "mournful solace," and finally there was a name to describe the atmosphere in my house. I tested the phrase on my best friend, Rosie Murray, one afternoon as we walked home from school. "How's your grandmom?" she'd asked. I said she wasn't getting better, then announced: "The house is filled with mournful solace." Rosie frowned and said, "I never know what you're talking about, but that sounds bad."

From Mersault I learned what "doing me dirt" meant and from the lines, "Really, nothing in my life had changed," I learned the supple art of irony. And sex? How erotic those scenes between Mersault and Marie, and how poignant her question, repeated three times, "Do you love me?" I would be a grown woman before I understood that the asking is the answer—"No." Later, Mersault's "callousness" would take on an aura of the heroic; how much less hope would be wasted on the unrequited if we could simply summon Mersault's direct, unapologetic, "No." Mostly, *The Stranger* showed me there were other ways to be and think, and although I would never become an "existentialist" save for a period in college when it seemed uncool not to be, I'd found a different narrative (one at odds with my deeply Catholic upbringing) for the meanings of God, death, guilt, and love.

On January 3, 1965, on a night as cold as Mersault's Algiers was hot, the ambulance arrived and the medics took my grandmother from her twin bed. The hard-packed snow outside glistened under the street lamp. Our cul-de-sac, always the last one plowed in our subdivision, was riven with icy tire tracks. After the commotion, on my way back to bed, I passed the bathroom and noticed her denture container, a fine pearly pink plastic, still sitting on the vanity. Without thinking, I grabbed it and ran outside in nothing but my blue nightgown, howling at the ambulance's red taillights, "You forgot her teeth!" But that was the last night I saw her alive.

In the months after the funeral, my grandmother's absence became the most palpable presence in my house. Unlike Mersault, my mother's mourning was visible, and her sorrow burst open at the oddest times: while baking a cake, or cleaning the living room. Bereft of ways to comfort her and bereft myself, I began writing at the kitchen table at night. I would wait until the house was so quiet even the electrical night-hum of the refrigerator and the heater kicking off seemed to stop. *The Stranger* was the model for a story called "The Hill," in which the sun—my sun—streamed, beat, bore down, pulsed, blazed, vibrated, and, in one gloriously dopey sentence, "sizzled on the sky's blue plate like a fried egg." In my black-and-white marbled copybook I began inventing people to fill the empty space real life and death had made in our home.

"With death so near, Mother must have felt like someone on the brink of freedom, ready to start life all over again," Mersault said at the end of *The Stranger*. And like him, as years passed and stories, then novels, spilled out of me, I, too, felt that with the creation of stories: "I laid my heart open to the benign indifference of the universe." A thief with a conscience, happily resigned to her life's penance: to be a writer.

LEE K. ABBOTT

The Most Daunting Book I Read
ABSALOM, ABSALOM! by William Faulkner

It is 1961, and your hero, at thirteen, doesn't know that he's having the perfect childhood for a writer: miserable.

He resides in Las Cruces, New Mexico (pop. 10,000 or so)—the southern, less chi-chi part of the state, the sky blue as poster paint, not a fruited plain in the area code, all paths from hither to yon thick with goatheads and snakeweed and walking stick cactus, a lot of Arizona real estate blowing his way during the spring.

His parents are divorced, and he and his younger brother live with their father, a retired army officer (three heart attacks: Adios, Uncle Sam), now a postal inspector (his job, it appears, is to preread *Playboy* magazine). His mother, a bleed-from-the-ears drunk, is locked up in the state hospital in Las Vegas and will be for another eight years, LSD among

Lee K. Abbott is the author of six collections of short stories, most recently *Wet Places at Noon*. He teaches at the Ohio State University in Columbus.

her many therapies (the major did try a private hospital in Roswell for some months, but she kept showing up on their doorstep, bottle of firewater in hand, eager to tell another whopper about venery and want and living beneath her station). The father's a drinker—Cuba Libres, mainly—and, Good Time Joe that he is, he's been known to drive home backward from the parties his set of swells likes to throw.

In brief, yours truly and his brother are being raised by the assistant golf pros, caddie master, and lifeguards at the country club, then a nine-hole track the boys all but bunk at. It's summer again, each day an oven on broil, and skinny Kit Abbott (it's short for Kittredge, Junior's middle name) is getting in and out of the low-octane trouble peculiar to an adolescent who has, according to every child psychologist and school counselor since second grade, thoroughly internalized the woe he's witnessed behind the front door of 1855 Cruse Avenue: He's been hysterically blind once; he's disfigured himself with a pair of scissors; he punched a girl classmate through a glass door at Alameda Elementary; during the fourth grade, he ran away from school every darn day; he's been caught shooting out street lights with fence staples; he's smoking Pall Mall cigarettes (grapevine, too); he's—well, he peeps routinely in Marci Hightower's window, and now, having survived the seventh grade, he's thinking about larceny and arson and bank robbing.

He wants to be a writer, but he doesn't know that yet either. Instead, he reads. Anything about Blackbeard the pirate. Books about sports heroes (he's a huge fan of Hammerin' Hank Aaron), not to mention all the magazines around the house—*Life, National Geographic, Golf Digest*. In the living room, he once found a copy of Hubert Selby's novel *Last Exit to Brooklyn* under the cushions of the couch—read that, too, disappointed that the dirty parts weren't dirty enough. Then, tired of the bounding main and ninth-inning hoopla, he started stealing cash out of his father's wallet: A bookstore had opened in town, Books Galore and More, and Kit, a dippy delinquent operating by instinct alone and profoundly bored by his own crummy company, found himself going through its doors one day.

Folks, I can't tell you how odd this bookstore was in my corner of "In-God-We-Trust-All-Others-Pay-Cash" America. On its shelves stood the *Paris Review* and the *Evergreen Review*, serious literary journals I'd one day seek to publish in. Arlene Belkin was the proprietress, her husband a physicist at New Mexico A&M (now New Mexico State University, from which I have two degrees related to the liar's art). Evidently, from the instant I'd crossed her threshold, she'd seen in me something that I, despite many hours in front of the mirror, had not yet seen myself. Maybe she was a sorceress come down to Planet Podunk to help me survive myself and one day type a story that would ravish a stranger the way a certain stranger's story was about to ravish me. I don't know. What I do know is that I gave her some money and—hocus-pocus—she gave me a book.

The Beggar by F. M. Esfandiary, then (so I recall from the dust jacket) Iran's diplomat to the United Nations. Think caftans, djinns, and a legless illiterate rolling down narrow, filth-clotted streets on a wooden platform with wheels. Think Camus without the ennui. The next week I received another by Mr. E., *Identity Card*. Think bureaucracy, Kafka in the Casbah, the absurd played out against a landscape as easily as forbidding as my own. Think the mysteries of selfhood.

Remember, please, that I was not choosing any of these titles. Instead, Arlene, having sized me up and doubtless thinking me a reed that needed to do a whole lot more thinking, went to her shelves for a volume that, like a magic carpet, was to whoosh me to an imagined world utterly unlike the world I had failed to imagine my way out of. The next book? Duck and cover, amigos, it's a doozy: *The*

Flowers by Jean Genet, notorious French thief and, gulp, practicing homosexual. Lord knows what this novel was to teach me. Maybe not to get caught. Maybe to stay out of France. Maybe the less-common needs of the heart. In any event, back the next week I went.

I'd heard of William Faulkner, sure. Long winded, I'd heard. No fan at all of going from A to B without a lot of visits to, say, L and R in between. Invented a county in Mississippi full of deviltry and decadence. Shoot, I might have heard that he had won the Nobel Prize. But I had not read a lick. Not a word. Until I took home—thank you, Arlene—*Absalom, Absalom!* (yes, do note the exclamation point, the fittest punctuation for a novel that from the get-go shouts about the only stuff worth shouting about—the fears and fluids of us, our crooked kith, our dire days, the sad dance we dance around the Truth).

So there I am at home, in my bedroom. (Think cowboy curtains and matching chenille bedspread. Think plaster-of-Paris hands clasped in prayer. Think hot rods on the bureau, fighter jets hanging on threads from the ceiling. Think a closet of clothes I didn't look cool enough in, and a summer day when I could lurk poolside at the country club ogling the comely Mrs. Fletcher.) And I am reading. Or trying to. The novel is open, I've heated up considerable gray matter making its acquaintance, but I've not gone much beyond the umpteen-umpteen paragraphs that Mr. F. takes to write "Once upon a time." What's slowing me down? Lordy, it's the words—the back and forth of an English I hadn't heard much at Heibert's Drive-In or the Piggly Wiggly.

"Circumambient," for example. "Effluvium." "Mote-palpitant." Plus, what was your teenage protagonist to make of the allusions to, say, Niobe and Thisbe and Pyramus? Faustus and Beelzebub, he was familiar with (the Abbotts were Episcopalians after all, believers in good grammar and expensive automobiles), but who, in these decidedly unenchanting acres of the Land of Enchantment, had ever heard of Carcassonne or "cold Cerberus" and the "palate-paunch" of Moloch? Nonetheless, something—call it narrative; no, call it, as Mr. Faulkner does, the "recounting which enables man to hear with living"—was driving yours truly forward. Instead of sneaking a peek at Miss Marci, I was sneaking more than a peek at Miss Merriam—Webster, that is. And at the Old Testament. Plus maps and a book about myths.

Clearly, I was enthralled, puzzling out what I could of this "horrible and bloody mischancing of human affairs," which a Vintage International edition curiously summarizes thus: "*Absalom, Absalom!* is the story of Thomas Sutpen and his ruthless, single-minded pursuit of his grand design—to forge a dynasty in Jefferson, Mississippi, in 1830—which is ultimately destroyed (along with Sutpen himself) by his own sons. A century later, the figure of Sutpen continues to haunt young Quentin Compson, who is obsessed with the legacy of Sutpen, and of the Old South." How lame.

Absalom, Absalom! is about "renegadery" and "the bitter purlieus of Styx." It's about the past that is never past, a present roiled with fear and lies. It has murder, near-incest, misogyny, miscegenation, mendacity, loves requited and those un-, War Civil and war familial. It's about "the time ladies did not walk but floated" and sounds that, although long gone, do still linger, "not as sound now but as something for the skin to hear, the hair on the head to hear." It's about an era "before it became fashionable to repair your mistakes by turning your back on them and running."

And, yes, it is about language, the purl and swirl of sentences that go as much backward in time as forward, monologues tangled as thickets, the talk talked between wight and welkin, the yarns of more modern sons of Ham, and the near-verse unique to "space and time and massy earth" themselves. Mr. Faulkner's English is "that scratch, that undying mark on the blank face of the oblivion to which we are all doomed." His is the imperishable prose about all that animates and beleaguers our terrible tribe, all that divides and unites us this side of the mool.

I am only semi-ashamed to admit that I did not finish that book that summer, nor for many summers after. Oh, I returned to it again and again—a moment here, a description there: Judith, Bon, Henry, and Sutpen less characters than spooky neighbors who had just left the room—but it wasn't until this summer that yours truly, a respectable adult nearly four decades distant from the vainglorious vandal he'd been, found himself with no more of its fifty-cent words to read, or to look up.

And then you know what I did? You guessed it: I opened the novel afresh, and, following that beginning one hundred thirty-one-word sentence (yeah, I counted), I was once again Quentin himself, on the verge of going off to Harvard in 1910, and sitting with Miss Rosa Coldfield for one "long still hot weary dead September afternoon" to hear a story about "acts of simple passion and simple violence, impervious to time and inexplicable . . . ," a story as much about here as there, as much about now as then.

SCOTT WEIDENSAUL

The Most Resonant Book I Read
A SAND COUNTY ALMANAC by Aldo Leopold

I was a weird kid—which wasn't, I now realize, quite as singular a fate as I thought when I was in junior high. But I still managed to isolate myself fairly well from most of my peers, by dint of an affinity for nature and wild animals that was tightly focused to the point of obsession.

I was one of those kids whose room their mother prefers not to clean, because she never knows what might be living under the bed. As I was much taken with snakes and salamanders in those days, she had grown used to finding shed garter snake skins entwined, like dry strips of cellophane, among the ribs of the old radiator beneath my window, or a lively black rat snake flowing effortlessly down the hallway to the stairs, having jimmied its way out of yet another supposedly escape-

· ·

Scott Weidensaul has written more than two dozen books on natural history, including *The Ghost with Trembling Wings: Science, Wishful Thinking, and the Search for Lost Species* and *Living on the Wind: Across the Hemisphere with Migratory Birds*, which was a finalist for the Pulitzer Prize.

proof cage. This was, frankly, more of a trial for my dad, who had a deathly fear of reptiles, than for my mother, whose phobias ran mostly to bats and small rodents.

Like my parents, adults tended to accept me, if with some bewilderment; I still wonder what the neighbors thought when they saw me one sweltering June day, wearing a heavy winter coat and my grandfather's hard hat, lugging a stepladder up into the woods that lapped the base of the adjacent mountain. (I'd found a Cooper's hawk nest, and I knew that when I climbed the tree for a peek, the angry female would strafe me bloody if I weren't well padded.)

Kids my own age were a different story. It's not as though I was friendless—I lived in the Pennsylvania countryside, where critter-collecting was a rite of passage—and I had neighborhood chums. But my tunnel vision about nature both accentuated and compensated for my social awkwardness at school, where I was clearly a geek—and not one of the bright, Honor Society geeks with their own clique, but just a peculiar, solitary kid who thought so long and hard about birds that he was perhaps not as aware of his outsider status as he might have been. Fortunately, in the tradition of weird, isolated kids everywhere, I had an epiphany—in my case, a slim book by a guy with a funny name, which changed my life in much the same way it changed our nation's relationship with the natural world. His opening words hit me right between my teenage eyes, and three decades haven't diminished their impact or their importance:

There are some who can live without wild things, and some who cannot. These essays are the delights and dilemmas of one who cannot. Like winds and sunsets, wild things were taken for granted until progress began to do away with them. Now we face the question whether a still higher "standard of living" is worth its cost in things

natural, wild and free. For us of the minority, the opportunity to see
geese is more important than television, and the chance to find a
pasque-flower is a right as inalienable as free speech.

By dang, I thought. That's me.

A Sand County Almanac by Aldo Leopold remains the most reso-
nant book I've read. I hold it close because it seems to have arms
wide enough to take in the entire world. It blends an unabashed passion for natural places and wild animals with a simple, clear logic
that argues for a more balanced relationship with the natural world.
Almanac is a classic work, and much more: It was the road map for
the more holistic conservation movement that emerged after World
War II, one embracing the fullness of biological diversity and natural
systems. It taught me the true meaning of belonging.

It is a book about connections—ecological connections, to be
sure, but it also gave me my first sense of connection to a wider
community, a validation of the passion I'd devoted to "things natural, wild and free," and the first recognition that such devotion could
be the work of a lifetime.

It also sparked an adolescent curiosity about this kindred spirit.
Aldo Leopold grew up in Iowa in the final years of the nineteenth
century, got a degree from Yale in the then-new discipline of
forestry, and headed West in 1909, to work in the resin-scented pine
woods of northern Arizona. By the 1920s, he'd been transferred by
the U.S. Forest Service to Wisconsin, but he was already growing
disillusioned with the commercial emphasis in forestry—the tree-
farm approach that viewed wild landscapes as just another commodity. An avid hunter, birder, angler, and all-around naturalist,
Leopold underwent an epiphany of his own in the 1930s, recogniz-
ing the astounding complexity of what he came to call "the land
organism," and the fundamental danger for any society that dealt

heedlessly with that complexity. He wrote groundbreaking books and articles on the new science of wildlife management, helped found the Wilderness Society in 1935, and began teaching ecology—a word little used even among scientists of the day—at the University of Wisconsin.

His refuge, through much of this time, was an old, played-out farm he and his wife bought in the so-called sand counties of central Wisconsin, which Leopold set out to restore to natural health. But he was looking beyond his students and professional colleagues, envisioning a series of ecological essays to bring the message to a wider public. After years of tinkering, false starts, and revisions—Knopf rejected it, suggesting he eliminate the ecological framework in favor of a collection of plain nature observations—Oxford University Press accepted the manuscript he called *Great Possessions* in April 1948, just days before Leopold died of a heart attack while fighting a grass fire on a neighbor's property.

The book, retitled by the publisher and edited by Leopold's son, Luna, came out the following year. Actually, what I (and most readers) think of as *A Sand County Almanac* is an amalgam—the original *Almanac,* plus essays from a second posthumous collection, *Round River,* published a few years later and eventually merged in a 1966 edition that remains the most common incarnation, and the one under whose spell I fell.

It is a deceptively simple book, especially in its opening sections; Leopold leads readers through a year on his old farm—the return of the geese, the sky-dance of courting woodcock, young white pines lancing up straight into the May sun. Much of this was familiar ground for me, growing up in the low hills of the central Appalachians with many of the same animals and plants, chasing grouse (as Leopold did) through October woods glowing with red blackberry leaves. Then the scenes shift to Mexico and the Southwest, to Canada and the North Wood, and here I was beguiled by the notion of exotic horizons that echoed with strange birdsong—a siren call, though I did not know it, that would eventually lead me all over the world. Like Leopold, I began to see my world not only as a tangle of local connections, but a web that embraced the globe, stitched together in ways as direct as the songbirds that nested in my yard and wintered in Guatemala, and as abstract as the flow of energy and atoms through a planetary organism.

But regardless of the setting, Leopold's vignettes are underpainted with a sometimes ferocious anger at what a negligent, self-indulgent society—especially the gear-crazed automobile culture fast gaining sway—was doing to once-wild landscapes. It was an anger I felt, but hadn't yet the vocabulary or experience to express. I'd already witnessed the small losses that are the common currency of naturalists—like the hundred acres of boggy forest near my home where I ran wild, hunting for ring-necked snakes and wood thrush nests, and where I first camped alone, which was leveled for new construction. I, who still had only the barest sense of natural science, already understood what Leopold meant when he said, "One of the penalties of an ecological education is that one lives alone in a world of wounds." *A Sand County Almanac* was, in many ways, the primer in my own ecological education, a template that my halting awareness recognized, and a framework within which it quickly grew.

Leopold was among the first scientists to articulate the necessity of treating the land like a single entity, not a series of disparate parts that could be husbanded or persecuted as if in a vacuum. Today, it may seem to be common sense to write, "Harmony with the land is like harmony with a friend; you cannot cherish his right hand and chop off his left." Yet in the 1940s, this was by no means a self-evident position, and most of his fellow game managers tried, for example, to boost popular game species like ducks and deer by exterminating predators like hawks and wolves. (Sadly, this mind-set is by no means entirely a thing of the past.)

Leopold himself passed through this stage, as an upstart forester in Arizona. In "Thinking Like a Mountain," he describes shooting a Mexican wolf as she fords a river with her pups, and he reaches her side in time to see "a fierce green fire" die in her eyes. "I was young then, and full of trigger-itch, and I thought that because fewer wolves meant more deer, that no wolves would mean hunters' paradise. But after seeing the green fire die, I sensed that neither the wolf nor the mountain agreed with such a view."

The expansiveness of Leopold's embrace is best seen through his writing's remarkable marriage of universality and specificity—the ultimate test of good nature writing, and a bar that he set very high. On one hand, his work is redolent of the upper Midwest—the slow-flowing rivers, the cornfields, and old woodlots, the tamarack swamps and crane marshes. There is an equal sense of place when he writes, with the evident fondness for youth's formative landscape, about the Southwest wilderness that he experienced from the saddle of a horse, or the melancholy that pervades "Song of the Gavilan," about a river in the Sierra Madre of Mexico where he first experienced unspoiled, aboriginal wilderness. The river changed his way of seeing the world, but he feared it was already doomed by encroaching civilization (as, sadly, it was; logging and grazing have degraded much of the Rio Gavilan).

As richly rendered as these places are in *A Sand County Almanac*, they are merely the backdrop against which Leopold introduces the core of his book, his heretical ideas about ecology, and forging a new, sustainable relationship between humanity and the land. "The last word in ignorance is the man who says of an animal or plant: 'What good is it?' If the land mechanism as a whole is good, then every part is good, whether we understand it or not. If the biota, in the course of aeons, has built something that we like but do not understand, then who but a fool would discard seemingly useless parts? To keep every cog and wheel is the first precaution of intelligent tinkering." Leopold, please note, was not against a little tinkering—he wasn't a hands-off purist—but no one has ever summed up the essence of conservation biology as succinctly or memorably.

In the essay "Goose Music," a piece that strikes a deep chord in me (for I am, like him, at once a birder, a hunter, a naturalist), Leopold muses on the comparative values—social, economic and even religious—of nature, and the bleakness of a world deprived of them:

To conclude: I have congenital hunting fever and three sons. As little tots, they spent their time playing with my decoys and scouring vacant lots with wooden guns. I hope to leave them good health, an education and possibly even a competence. But what are they going to do with these things if there be no more deer in the hills, and no more quail in the coverts? No more snipe whistling in the meadows, no more piping of widgeons and chattering of teal as darkness covers the marshes; no more whistling of swift wings as the morning star pales in the east? And when the dawn-wind stirs through the ancient cottonwoods, and the gray light steals down from the hills over the old river sliding softly past its wide brown sandbars—what if there be no more goose music?

A world without goose music was a vivid prospect in Leopold's time, and no less so now, in this age of global biological erosion, when we are told that three or four species an hour disappear into the maw of extinction. The "world of wounds" can become too much for an aging naturalist, and now that I'm in my forties, I've accumulated my own Rio Gavilans, my own poignant landscapes of loss.

Not long ago, I spent some time kicking around the sand coun-

ties of central Wisconsin, a land of oak woods, dairy farms, and fragments of tallgrass prairie, which seemed profoundly familiar to me
from the pages of that book. In Leopold's day, the marshes here—
what few hadn't been drained for farming—were home to a beleaguered handful of sandhill cranes, to him one of the most potent
symbols of wild America. In "Marshland Elegy," one of my favorite
Almanac essays, Leopold writes, "Our ability to perceive quality in
nature begins, as in art, with the pretty. It expands through succes-
sive stages of the beautiful to values as yet uncaptured by language.
The quality of cranes lies, I think, in this higher gamut, as yet
beyond the reach of words."

Leopold had little hope that Wisconsin would save its remnant
cranes, which numbered only a few dozen in his day. He told friends,
in the years just before his death, to cherish the sight and sound of
the great birds, the "pandemonium of trumpets, rattles, croaks, and
cries that almost shakes the bog with its nearness," for they soon
would be gone—a sentiment he echoed in the final passage of the
essay. "Some day . . . the last crane will trumpet his farewell and spi-
ral skyward from the great marsh. High out of the clouds will fall the
sound of hunting horns, the baying of the phantom pack, the tinkle
of little bells, and then a silence never to be broken, unless perchance
in some far pasture of the Milky Way." But thanks in large measure to
the new, embracive approach to conservation that Leopold made so
vivid, so compelling, the marshes still echo to the "pandemonium of
trumpets" each spring. And not just a few, but a great roar—eleven
thousand sandhill cranes that crowd the bogs and soggy meadows of
Wisconsin and move in great echelons against the sky, a living affirmation that with a little direction, humanity can sometimes bridge
the gulf between itself and the wild world.

FREDERICK BUSCH

The Most Dangerous Book I Read

THE DARING YOUNG MAN ON THE FLYING TRAPEZE AND OTHER STORIES by William Saroyan

A young person who will go on to write is someone who, because of books that draw him, retreats to a room or a quiet place or, in a stormy house, the slightest shelter in the storm; there, he exercises the muscles of imagination. He will— among, say, Al Avery's A Yankee Flier series, the Grosset & Dunlap *Arabian Nights*, or Eric Ambler's *Coffin for Dimitrios*— discover one book that demands he go beyond his reading and try to write, and mean it. That is his great and dangerous book.

It will not necessarily be a book about writing. Perhaps it will be something like Ernie Pyle's reports on World War II in *Brave Men*, which caused me to wonder how he made me want to weep, when I was eleven years old, about people I had

....

Frederick Busch has published twenty-five books, including *The Night Inspector* and *A Memory of War*. He is a recipient of the Award of Merit from the American Academy of Arts and Letters and the PEN/Malamud Award in Short Fiction. He lives in upstate New York.

never met. I looked through those dutiful and heroic lives, and I saw the glow of the furnaces that powered writing.

It could be, for a high school or college student, a huge short story such as "Down at the Dinghy" in J. D. Salinger's great collection *Nine Stories*. That is the one about a little boy who, used to living in his imagination, hears, with touching inaccuracy, his parents' housekeeper calling his father a kike. The boy runs away, mostly in his imagination, and the kid who is going to be a writer will be as moved by Salinger's evocation of the boy's mother, Boo Boo Tannenbaum, as by her little boy's plight. How did he do that, the infected kid will wonder.

Or he will come upon—as I did, in my parents' bookshelves, among their left-wing brochures and a novel by Albert Maltz and Alberto Moravia's *A Woman of Rome*, a dangerous little volume in, I think, a Modern Library edition of 1934. It was by William Saroyan, and it was called *The Daring Young Man on the Flying Trapeze and Other Stories*. I think of it as the beginning of my passionate and humbling affair with the American short story.

First of all, there was the preface by this man of whom I'd never heard. He told me that in studying "all the classic rules" governing the short story, he learned that "they had been leaving me out, and as far as I could tell I was the most important element in the matter, so I made some new rules."

His humor here, as throughout the collection, is a little heavy handed and very true. His own beliefs about the making of the short story—something I'd never dreamed just anyone could sit around and do—boiled down to this: "Forget everybody who ever wrote anything." That's dangerous advice for a kid, not only because a serious writer cannot entirely mean it, as we are formed not only in rebellion against our tradition, but equally by our longtime loyalty to aspects of it; the advice is dangerous because it is precisely what a

kid will want to believe. He was born to believe it. The wars of adolescence are fought over variations of this instruction, and civil
wars—the writer's childish id versus his well-educated superego—
characterize plenty of the so-called mature years in a working
writer's life.

He joked in his preface that he now doesn't bother about rules
at all: "I just sit down and write. Now and then I stand and write."
But I somehow knew, and every working writer knows, that jokes
aren't only funny, and that, like the best ones, this one was true.
Saroyan was defining a writer, who is someone who writes. There
are people who talk about writing, and people who talk about writers, and then there are the writers: You can tell who they are
because they are the ones who are either standing and writing or sitting and writing; the others talk about it, but the writers write. I
knew this from Saroyan when I first encountered his book in my
early adolescence, and I know it to be true in these, the days of my
somewhat later adolescence.

I surely did not understand this paragraph, which contains
Saroyan's notions on style:

*A writer can have, ultimately, one of two styles: He can write in a man-
ner that implies that death is inevitable, or he can write in a manner that
implies that death is not inevitable. Every style ever employed by a writer
has been influenced by one or another of these attitudes toward death.*

Kids think that "style" is about verve—how you show that you
have drunk of the blood of Conrad, or partaken of the substantiating
flesh of William Faulkner. It's the elders who know that how you
write what you write is about time—what Saroyan, at twenty-six,
called "death," which as a nickname will suffice. He ended his preface with advice. He was always, in his fiction and in his drama and

in his essays, giving advice; it was what charmed a reader, or sent the reader mumbling away. "Try to be alive," the young author counseled. "You will be dead soon enough."

This was from a man who knew of the Turkish genocide of the Armenians, and this was from a man who wrote in the Great Depression. This was from a man who believed in the victory by death, but who wished not to. This man wrote stories in which, like his eponymous character "Harry" in one of the stories, he tried to reinvent himself—"making things pop, a real American go-getter." And it was this American voice that spoke to me, the big-mouthed, well-educated, carefully tended, too-well-nourished American boy of Russian- and Austrian-Jewish extraction, with a six-inch pompadour held in place with Vaseline, who rolled his sleeves very high to show the muscles he didn't quite have, and whose brain could not help trying to make stories.

The title story of the book made an impression—a deep indentation, a literary canyon. First, it was full of the gorgeous music I had not learned was permissible in prose. Poetry, I thought, could be pretty, while prose had to be serviceable. Not so, Saroyan instructed. In the first part of "The Daring Young Man on the Flying Trapeze," we meet the protagonist through his mind. I had never heard of Joyce or Faulkner, and I had read only action scenes in Hemingway, and one reverie in "The Snows of Kilimanjaro," which I liked for its reference to lovemaking. But here came the voice of the mind, whether I was ready or not. Here came: "Horizontally wakeful amid universal widths, practicing laughter and mirth, satire, the end of all, of Rome and yes of Babylon, clenched teeth, remembrance . . . the roar of Dostoyevsky, and the dark sun." I could feel that final rhythmic shift, and I knew, although in ignorance, that I was hearing someone's mind. So you could describe a character from within, I learned; and you could do so with a kind of language music.

And then, I learned, as I read on, you could make a character who was neither a soldier nor baseball player. You could make someone on the page who was somehow equally heroic: a writer.

In "The Daring Young Man on the Flying Trapeze," this writer is starving. He applies for a job. His interviewer asks—on Saroyan's pages, these exchanges are without quotation marks, so they feel as if they occur within minds as well as in the open air of the world: Now tell me . . . what can you do? I can write, he said pathetically. She doesn't understand what he means. Write what? she asks, almost angrily. Prose, he said simply.

And at this point the Kafka in us all has risen in me, and I am raging against the bureaucracy of existence, but also this awareness: The person at the center of the conversation and action in this story, someone who must either take up the cudgel or be cudgeled, is a writer of prose. I was not alone in what I wished to do—true, I had wanted to be a space commando, a member of the Civil Air Patrol, a lawyer like my father as well as a forest ranger; but I had wanted, withal, to hang around, not taking too many orders, and write—and, furthermore, I was not alone in my suspicion that my yearnings were, and would be labeled, socially useless.

The nameless hero of Saroyan's story is light headed with hunger and cold. Actual life and death are part of the story, accompanying, on every page and in every paragraph, the protagonist's insistence upon the glories of language well made. We conclude with him in his bare room. He has pawned his watch, and his books, and his best suit. There is nothing left to sell. He is filled with anger "to think that there was no respect for men who wrote." It is the importance of writing, and not fear for his life, that dominates here as he seems, before our eyes, to die. He has gone through his tortured day singing to himself the song about the daring young man on the flying trapeze who floats through the air with the greatest of ease. He polishes the one penny in his possession, and he reads it, he celebrates the face of Lincoln—it is the face of America—and "In God We Trust Liberty 1923": "How beautiful it is," he said, speaking not only of liberty, circumscribed or not, but also of language.

"Then swiftly, neatly, with the grace of the young man on the trapeze, he was gone from his body," I read.

I remember thinking: Hold it. The guy just died. Perhaps it was the first story I read in which the hero died. Surely, it was the start of my considering that I had choices about whether my own heroes would live. It was the beginning of my long lesson in how the beating of an actual heart is at the heart of telling true stories.

I had just read about dying for art. I had just read about a society that was accused of letting its artists die. I had read an adult story in a grown-up book about the rebellious child who threatens to die if he isn't permitted to win his skirmish with the world of rules; and, in that story, the world of rules had let the rebel die. I was shocked. Moreover, I was threatened. If I wished to be such a rebel, I would have to accept the double-edged threat. I was unafraid because I was young, imperceptive, and a little stupid about danger, which I knew from books and from quick beatings in the Flatbush playgrounds from which I nicely recovered. I forgot the danger soon enough, I think, retaining the romantic glow, the operatic appeal, of showing them all by dying for art, as long as I didn't have to suffer. Lessons about that aspect of the profession came later.

I turned to the next story, "Seventy Thousand Assyrians," and found that you could write American stories in a vernacular, American voice: "I hadn't had a haircut in forty days and forty nights, and I was beginning to look like several violinists out of work." This speaker was also a writer—"rejected story from Scribner's, rejected essay from the *Yale Review*, no money for decent cigarettes, worn shoes, old shirts." Of course, I didn't know that I was reading a description that would be true of me in 1962 and 1963, but I did sense that some of the glow of glory I perceived around the shoulders of Saroyan's heroes had to do with their suffering, and of course I was enchanted, for I saw myself as a young fellow infinitely capable of very attractive suffering.

And I was enchanted, too, because I was a little precocious, and I did sense that someone who knew about it was telling me truths concerning the language of American storytelling: "I am not out to win the Pulitzer Prize," says a character created by this writer who would later win the honor but refuse to accept it. "I am out here in the far West, in San Francisco, in a small room on Carl Street, writing a letter to common people, telling them in simple language things they already know."

And I was hooked. You didn't have to know a lot that was new, apparently: You needed to have strong feelings, and a voice with which to make them heard; and then you got—once you were a writer, whether successful or not—to tell things to people. Sign me up!

That this story also was about the murder of the Armenians did not escape me. I was a war baby, born in 1941, and alert to killing and to actual killing grounds. But what thrilled me, I have to confess, was not the sadly familiar news about the executions of the innocent. It was the love song to and about writing I heard in Saroyan's words. In "Myself upon the Earth," the story ends with a writer recovering his typewriter. "It is before me now," he writes, "and I am tapping at it, and this"—the story before us—"is what I have written." Writing, and the American language, were what the stories celebrated. They praised love and generosity, they complained bitterly "because the existence of hatred and ugliness in the heart of man is a truth," they lavished sweet attention upon the glories of San Francisco and upon sad Jews and victimized girls and honest men.

And they praised the writer and his art by making him a subject of stories. "Early this morning," he writes in "A Cold Day," "when I was warm with coffee I had this great story in my mind, ready to get into print, but it got away from me.

"The most I can say now," he concludes, "is that it is very cold in San Francisco today, and I am freezing."

The writer in the act of writing: a new literary hero, and dangerous to boys such as I was, who grew up or, anyway, continued, and who became—in part because of this man's sweet, serious example—the writer I must confess to being.

ROBERT MORGAN

The Wisest Book I Read

DOCTOR ZHIVAGO by Boris Pasternak

In the late summer of 1959 I was preparing to enter the tenth grade at Flat Rock High in Henderson County, North Carolina. My sister was getting ready to enter college, and my parents drove us down to Greenville, South Carolina, in the pickup truck one day to buy school clothes. I had saved money from selling pole beans, and in the air-conditioned stores I bought new pants with buckles in the back, new shirts, a pair of white buck loafers, and a belt as thin as a shoelace. Before driving back to the mountains, we stopped in a drugstore near the parking lot for cold drinks. Near the marble fountain counter was a rack of paperback books.

While sipping my Coke, I turned the rack, reading titles. One black and red Mentor caught my attention: *Doctor Zhivago* by Boris Pasternak, a book that had been much in the news

Robert Morgan is a professor of English at Cornell University. He has published eight works of fiction, including the novel *Gap Creek*, and ten books of poems, including *Topsoil Road*.

during the past year. There had been a scandal about Pasternak
being forced to refuse the Nobel Prize. I had heard the book was a
love story, critical of the Russian Revolution and the Soviet regime.
Before leaving the drugstore I paid ninety-five cents for the volume,
the first book I ever bought.

I had already fallen in love with Tolstoy's fiction, devouring a
copy of *War and Peace* borrowed from the Henderson County book-
mobile. And I had read *Crime and Punishment* in a tattered paperback sent to a friend by his brother in college. I had also written my
first paper the year before on *Quo Vadis?* I was in awe of Russian fiction, of Slavic romance. I could hardly wait to get home with the
inky-smelling paperback.

I was not disappointed by Pasternak's novel. I read it at odd
moments between field work and homework, milking the cow and
helping to make molasses. I thought it was the wisest story I'd ever
read. It was a love story, and the poetic prose, the sweeping scenes
of the countryside and city, train rides and devastated towns, were
so real it hurt to read them. The feeling for field and forest, river and
ravine, decaying house and ruined backstreet, seemed a revelation.
Even as I wrestled with the chopped-up narrative sections, the awk-
wardly joined chapters and the literary allusions beyond my understanding, I was thrilled by the details of muddy roads, snowy vistas,
clothing shops, ballrooms, and smoldering battlefields.

And over the chaos of the revolution, the threatened lives of Yuri
the poet and Tonia his wife, and Lara his muse and lover, there hung
a spell of sacredness, of destiny. I couldn't have described the sense
of luminous presence in the story then, but I recognized it and was
thrilled by it. The details of the novel, the pain of the story, the
entwined lives of the heroes, had a special meaning, beyond anything I could have defined. I understood something about the political history the book revealed and implied. But it was the lives and

loves of the individuals projected against that cataclysmic history that enthralled me. History was a beast that devoured those precious lives. I missed the references to Baudelaire and Mayakovski, but I understood the celebration of poetry as simplicity, the immanence of the everyday, the complex textures of modern life illuminated by goodness, simple purity of heart.

More than any book I had ever read, *Doctor Zhivago* made me feel I was touching real life. I saw that the true subject of fiction, and poetry, was the dignity and spirituality of human life in harsh circumstances. Other writers had said the same thing, but it was Pasternak who drove home the lesson to me, in his uneven and somewhat disjointed masterpiece.

Doctor Zhivago was my first encounter with that special genre, the flawed masterwork. Later I would come to know *The Adventures of Huckleberry Finn, The Charterhouse of Parma,* and *Tender Is the Night.* But then I believed what a teacher had told me, that great art was about perfection of form. *Doctor Zhivago* showed me that great writing can succeed in spite of its imperfections. No other work would touch me in quite the same way. I read Pasternak at just the right time.

One of the special messages *Doctor Zhivago* sent to me was that poetry and prose fiction were complementary, not antithetical. In American writing, the two genres are almost always separate. Of the classic American prose writers, only Melville and Poe wrote notable poetry. But the hero of Pasternak's novel is a poet, like the author, and a great poet. And many of the discussions in the story are about poetry and the place of poetry in modern life. The novel might be the first work of literary criticism I ever read. It is still one of the best discussions of poetry I know. More important, the book ended with a selection of Zhivago's poems. I will never forget reading "Hamlet," "Bad Roads in Spring," and "Hopbines" there. The concluding poem, "Garden of Gethsemane," taught me something about the possibilities of poetry, just when I was most impressionable. The poem ends:

"Seest thou, the passing of the ages is like a parable
And in its passing it may burst to flame.
In the name, then, of its awesome majesty
I shall, in voluntary torments, descend into my grave.

I shall descend into my grave. And on the third day rise again.
And, even as rafts float down a river,
So shall the centuries drift, trailing like a caravan,
Coming for judgment, out of the dark, to me."

I might have missed many of the literary allusions, but I certainly got the biblical references. I had been raised by Fundamentalists who read the Bible to my sister and me every day. I understood that the poems were a homage to a church and belief that had been virtually wiped out by the Soviet regime. The novel was a monument, in part, to a world now lost, to the church, to artists and thinkers purged and lost, to the poet/Christ figure of Zhivago.

I realized that Pasternak had written, not only to honor those lost, but to celebrate sanity and health, the human potential, against the devastation of totalitarianism and ideology. It was only later, as I studied Russian poetry and history, that I saw what an elegy Pasternak had written for particular Russian futurists and symbolists, such as Blok and Mayakovski. I also came to see the book as a lament for the legacy of the church, the culture that had been preserved and handed down by so many generations until 1918. Pasternak's feeling for the meaning of tradition moved me more than Eliot's essays and poems would.

Reading *Doctor Zhivago* helped me see how fiction and poetry make the world, and history, immediate, palpable. I saw that novels were about details, surprise, unexpected truths. More important, they were about lives, and they helped us to see the gift of family legacy and church that so many had worked to create for us. The story of loss and suffering was really a celebration of the things around me I hadn't noticed before. The novel showed me the privileges I had enjoyed and the importance of humility and compassion. The book showed me something of my own failures and limitations.

I never forgot the description of revising a poem on page 453. Pasternak describes how Zhivago's poems to Lara, written in the most desperate, hopeless time, go through draft after draft, until they are no longer just a personal statement but a work of art that speaks to all. Of this essential paradox about writing, the narrator says:

As a result, his feeling, still pulsing and warm, was gradually eliminated from his poems, and romantic morbidity yielded to a broad and serene vision that lifted the particular to a level of the universal and familiar. He was not deliberately striving for such a goal, but this broad vision came of its own accord as a consolation, like a message sent to him by Lara from her travels, like a distant greeting.

Oddly enough, the passage that made the deepest impression on me was one of the most obscure, the section describing Zhivago's return to Moscow by foot and rail across a Russia ruined by war and revolution. The chapters are a catalog of towns and countryside torn by war, disease, dislocation. I read it again and again for its detail and panoramic sweep. I felt in my heart that Pasternak was teaching me about history and culture and what it means to be human, more than any textbook or Sunday school had:

In unharvested fields the ripe grain spilled and trickled on the ground. Yuri Andreievich gathered it in handfuls, and at the worst, if he had no means of boiling it and making gruel, he stuffed it into his mouth and chewed it with great difficulty. The raw, half-chewed grain was almost indigestible.

Particular books affect us at particular times. Each of us finds our own literary canon. I found *Doctor Zhivago* at just the right time, for it showed me how fiction brings the world to our own eyes and breath and connects us intensely with those so different, so distant, and yet so much like ourselves. I saw how much I had to learn and, just as important, I saw how much I already knew without knowing it.

ERIC WRIGHT

The Classiest Book I Read
HOWARDS END by E. M. Forster

Just before my eldest sister got married, there were ten children, two parents, and a pair of books living under our one roof.

One of those books was a novel by Ouida, the pronunciation of whose name fascinated me when I began to learn to read. I don't know where it came from. Perhaps my father "found" it in the back of his van after one of the removal jobs he used to do when he wasn't delivering frozen beef from the London docks to the warehouses. It certainly wasn't bought; by the time I was six we had risen to join the lower–working class, having just escaped from the underclass, the London poor, but no one at our level had the money to buy books.

The other volume was a William book by Richmal Crompton, *Just William,* I think. I don't know where this book

. . . .

Eric Wright is the author of seventeen mysteries, a comic novel, a collection of short stories, *A Killing Climate*, and a memoir about growing up in south London and emigrating to Canada, *Always Give a Penny to a Blind Man*.

came from, either. Many of the pages were missing, some had been torn, and all the illustrations had been scribbled on by me and my young sister before we could read. My earliest memory concerning books is of my brother, at about eight, trying to teach me to read by pointing at one of the illustrations and asking me to read the caption. "Johnny steals the cakes," was my guess at one, an answer that so tickled him that for a while I said it when he pointed at any of the illustrations.

Soon I really could read the captions, and then the text, and found out that Johnny was really William, and he was, indeed, stealing the cakes. The next step was to get a sister to take me to the municipal library where I found all the rest of the William books.

Read at the right age, they are endearing and funny books; the hero, William Brown, was someone I could admire and want to be. William, whose father worked "in the City" and whose mother employed a cook, belonged to the solid middle class, which from my point of view might just as well have been the aristocracy. I loved reading about this world but I made no connection between it and my own. Richmal Crompton wrote comic realism for middle-class children; for me and my kind she actually wrote fairy stories.

It is a truism now that nearly all children's literature in England before World War II was written by and for the middle classes. Christopher Robin, Peter Pan, *The Wind in the Willows* are all products of their authors' childhoods, but for me and my kind, they were romances, made so by being set in another country—the land of nannies, housemaids, and cooks.

By the time I was eleven, Cockney children who had won scholarships to grammar schools were making jokes about this middle-class literature. "I say," we would say, in what we believed was an upper-class accent, "Shall we go to the tuck shop and spend the money order my mater sent me?" which was code for, "Let's go and buy some suckers; I've got three ha'pence my mum gave me." We were not making fun of this world; we loved it.

Around age twelve, I was taken over by the simpler forms of thrillers. They had such heroes as The Saint and Bulldog Drummond and I slurped them up like a drunkard. Then literary realism appeared, first at school in the form of approved novels by Galsworthy and Hugh Walpole, whose world was real to our teachers, which qualified them to be called realism. But for us, any story with servants in it, any imitation of middle-class life, was still set in another country, still a kind of romance.

At about fifteen, I, along with my friends, began to reject this world in favor of another, the one portrayed by Theodore Dreiser, Sinclair Lewis, John Steinbeck, and Ernest Hemingway, the (to us) classless world of American literature. We were living in south London, but felt at home in their world in a way that we no longer did in the one depicted in the English novels we were supposed to admire for their truth to nature. After Hemingway, even Somerset Maugham felt quaint, musty, old fashioned. And so I went on my mindless way, neither acquiring nor needing the critical vocabulary to articulate why I had abandoned English storytellers in favor of Americans.

Much has been written on the English class system and on the experiences of the scholarship boys of sixty years ago, their attempts to achieve successful lives within the enmeshing confines of their class, lives in which questions of background, accent, and manners clung like brambles to the young travelers making their way through the undergrowth to the class above them. I can only echo the wonderful remark of Peter De Vries. "My childhood was as unhappy as the next braggart's." I felt paralyzed by my circumstances and saw no hope of changing them.

Certainly I couldn't escape my world by moving up, so I moved out. I emigrated to Canada, to the continent, if not the country, of my reading. Much of the thrust to leave my world behind was instinctive, prompted by an unoriginal desire to remake myself, but the path of the eventual remaking was back and down into my roots, finding there the knowledge I needed to come into my own. Fleeing from my heritage, I was then given a chance to embrace it, something made easier by having moved away from it first.

The beginnings of an understanding of what I had done and why, did not begin to become apparent to me until I took a course at the University of Manitoba. The topic was T. S. Eliot's poem "A Cooking Egg." When we came to the final lines, "Weeping, weeping multitudes / Droop in a hundred A.B.C.'s" the professor asked us to consider the idea of a child's primer and a world of young children all crying over their lessons.

This, I saw, was rubbish, and for the first time in my life I was the only person in the room who could prove it. I should have been more diffident, for the professor was fond of his insight, but I was too happy and said immediately, "But, sir, A.B.C. means Aerated Bread Company." This company operated a chain of genteel teashops in London at this time and the reference was to the sadness of the lonely young women whom Eliot had seen in them.

The professor, caught, snapped, "What on earth has the Aerated Bread Company to do with the poetry of Eliot?" looking at the other students for support.

I explained, and had then to watch him, to my sorrow, flounder about trying to connect my A.B.C.s to his, but he couldn't do it, and he never forgave me.

Nevertheless, I was alerted to the realization that I might have some tiny original experience to bring to bear on a text. The Eliot episode had emboldened me; the real breakthrough came when we were assigned *Howards End* by E. M. Forster. I saw that for the first time I was in a unique position, alone among my friends from the Canadian prairie in being able to point out that this author's work, or some aspect of it, was vitiated by his ignorance of other classes, particularly the lower classes. I began, in other words to create a critical understanding of writers whom I had already rejected by instinct. I knew what working-class people were like, and most of the writers on the approved list didn't.

Howards End is a story of the meeting of two worlds, the practical real world of businessman Henry Wilcox and his family, a world of "telegrams and anger"; and the world of the Schlegel sisters, Margaret and Helen, and their brother Tibby, a world that prizes personal relations and the inner life, the world of the spirit. The novel is driven by its epigraph, "Only connect. . . ." The theme is the need to connect the two worlds, the Wilcoxes and the Schlegels, to make one whole. Margaret bears the burden of connecting these two worlds by marrying Henry Wilcox. At first she fails, and then through the consequences of a tragic accident that kills a young clerk, Leonard Bast, whom the sisters have befriended, the bridge is built, the connection is made and the realms of "the prose and the passion" become one.

The book had alerted me to its problem in the beginning. I was not alone in finding the working out of the novel's theme in the marriage of Margaret Schlegel and Wilcox unconvincing, but I was alone in my response to Leonard Bast. But by now I had acquired some courage.

I had developed several chips on my shoulder over the portrayal of the English working classes in fiction, exempting only *Sons and Lovers*. Eliot's distaste for the typist and her seduction in *The Waste Land*, distastefully told, told me something about Eliot. I tried to find a single critic (this was 1953) who found Eliot's disgust unattractive, elitist, and fastidious to the point of inhuman. At the other pole, I was tired of fiction's warm-hearted Cockneys, covered in pearl buttons.

But Leonard Bast was more important than these. Here was a character with exactly my background, put into a novel to create a plot, to bring the Schlegels and Wilcoxes together. Whether the device works, and I don't think it does, Leonard Bast never becomes more than a badly made puppet.

The core of the problem is that Bast is a member of the clerical lower class, about as fiercely respectable a stratum of society as has ever existed, entirely dependent on appearances to keep them above the classless no-man's-land below, who is living with a woman to whom he is not married. Now for Bast to live in sin, and risk its being known (he would be sacked immediately) is unthinkable. It is a relationship that Forster found in his own experience, that of the Bloomsbury circle, and moved down the scale to where it would never be tolerated. For society—in this case, the neighbors— to accept Bast and his mistress they would have to have moved even lower in the scale, to what we now call the underclass, the class my grandparents came from, where nobody cares. (My grandmother sold flowers around the London pubs to support the household.)

Bast, as a clerk, has his feet on the bottom rung of the class ladder, and he would never have risked slipping off. Brooding thus on the character, I thought about his name. All the other names in the novel are familiar sounding, English or German, but Bast is unusual enough to look as if Forster might have made it up. It has no literary associations that I know of, and I have never come across it in life, though there are several in the Toronto telephone directory. I suspect Forster invented the name to avoid associations, as he invented the character in order to kill him off without too much grief; Bast dies as he lived, in an unlikely fashion, to serve Forster's plot.

Forster's attempt to portray someone from another class defeated him, and the failure makes the novel creak. All of his characters then become questionable, and their relationships, especially that of Margaret and Wilcox, become somewhat artificial when tested against the real world. Wilcox has to be crippled by his son's imprisonment (for the manslaughter of Bast) to be made human enough to be a fit partner for Margaret. In fact the only character who behaves in a way that is consistent and entirely believable is Tibby, who becomes in the end, as Margaret says, "somewhat a dear." Everyone else performs the role Forster has allotted to them, to validate the novel's thesis.

In 2001, I interviewed in public the Tibetan writer Jamyang Norbu. Toward the end of the interview, in order to engage the audience a bit, I asked him to say a word about writers on India whom the audience might know, Kipling and Forster, for example. Much to my surprise, he said that his Indian friends adored Kipling. "Kipling understood India," he said.

And Forster? *A Passage to India*?

"Oh no," he said. "Forster never understood India at all."

This isn't good literary criticism, of course; it's gossip and prejudice. I think it's probably true, though. I think *Howards End* is a failure because of Forster's inability to portray someone of a lower class. I'm not surprised to learn that some Indians feel him to have understood as little of the subtleties of Indian society as he did of the English working class. As he did of people like me.

ANTHONY WALTON

The Most Eloquent Book I Read
ROCK SPRINGS by Richard Ford

I was lying on my bed in a dormitory at the University of Notre Dame, idling away a cold winter Saturday by reading *Esquire,* a magazine I was proud of myself for being aware of, as it seemed to cater to a certain kind of sophisticated and debonair man—well off enough to drive a BMW, cool enough to listen to Miles Davis, and deep enough to appreciate serious literature. That was how I saw myself that afternoon, or at least how I saw myself becoming in the years after I finished school, if I ever finished school there on the cold prairie of Indiana, watched over by priests and nuns and severe professors.

The short stories were toward the back of the magazine. I preferred the lifestyle pieces—the comparative advantages of

....

Anthony Walton is a poet, essayist, and critic who lives in Brunswick, Maine. He is the author of the memoir/history *Mississippi: An American Journey* and the poetry collection *Cricket Weather* and an editor of the *Vintage Book of African American Poetry*. Walton, who teaches English at Bowdoin College, was a 1998 recipient of the Whiting Writers Award.

tropical blend versus gabardine, the proper way to drink vermouth. But this particular story grabbed me as I skimmed the first couple of lines: "Edna and I had started down from Kalispell, heading for Tampa–St. Pete where I still had some friends from the old glory days who wouldn't turn me in to the police." The driving verbal rhythm of these lines continues, through the story of the ex-con Earl, on the lam and rolling for Florida with his girlfriend in a stolen cranberry red Mercedes, through dangers and disappointments and onto the now-classic finish that strangely and magically turns the whole thing back onto the reader: "What would you think a man was doing if you saw him in the middle of the night looking in the windows of cars in the parking lot of the Ramada Inn? Would you think he was trying to get his head cleared? Would you think he was trying to get ready for a day when trouble would come down on him? Would you think his girlfriend was leaving him? Would you think he had a daughter? Would you think he was anybody like you?"

I was twenty-one years old, and cannot claim to have appreciated the profound humanity of these lines. What grabbed me was the language of *Rock Springs*. This was it, as far as I, a novice poet, was concerned. I thought to myself, after my first reading of *Rock Springs,* that to write one thing like that would constitute happiness and the conclusion of a satisfying writing career.

I started hunting down stories by this fellow, Ford, which in pre-internet days was not the easiest of tasks. I bought the hardcover *Rock Springs* on the day it first appeared in stores, at a time of my life when eighteen dollars was no small expenditure. I would loaf during my job as an elevator man in a building just down the street from the United Nations, reading the stories again and again. Ford could make you feel like you were standing on a forlorn, windswept prairie, staring off at the snow-capped mountains in the distance: "The sunset that day I remember as being the prettiest I'd ever seen.

Just as it touched the rim of the horizon, it all at once fired the air into jewels and red sequins the precise likes of which I had never seen before and haven't seen since." As I read and studied and memorized, I became deeply excited to learn how one word, like "precise" in the foregoing quotation, could tip the balance in a sentence and send it into orbit.

And the unique fit of Ford's language with his subject matter opened to me a world of possibility. Ford and other writers at the time, like Raymond Carver, Tobias Wolff, and Joy Williams, were stretching subject matter into places—trailer parks, truck stops, gold mines, the interior lives of society's losers—often not thought fit for the highest pitch of American language. Ford's elegiac treatment of common lives, his drawing on Shakespearean rhythms and the rhetoric of the King James Version of the Bible, helped me to realize that things in my own life were subject matter, things in my own family and my own past that I would have thought too small or too humble to make literature.

In 1989, through a series of happy accidents, I was given an opportunity to write an essay for the *New York Times Magazine*, "Willie Horton and Me"—an essay that gained some notoriety because of its complaint that all black males were being painted with the brush of the rapist and murderer who had been featured in campaign commercials on behalf of George H. W. Bush. It was the first thing I had ever written that felt like it came from me. I look back now at the flourishes and pretensions of some of my earlier attempts at writing, and then at the plainspoken English of that essay, and I can't help but think of the lessons I had learned from Ford's stories about the relation, for a writer, of rhetoric to experience. I was learning that true eloquence was born at the point where those two things met—where the emotion is real and strong enough to be worthy of the highest pitch of language, and where the language does not seek to embellish or amplify, but rather to name the true contours of that emotion. I was learning to say what I thought and felt. Looking back on it, what is perhaps most intriguing to me is that, though "Willie Horton and Me" dealt with some of the most painful racial issues of our time, my learning to speak about it had as much to do with what I had learned from *Rock Springs* as it did with what I'd learned from, say, a great black essayist like James Baldwin. Young writers, I think, learn from everything they read; American writers, of whatever background, own all of what's out there.

After I had written a few more pieces in New York, I was given an opportunity to write a book, which became *Mississippi: An American Journey*. Between that point and my sitting on my bed in South Bend reading *Rock Springs*, I had spent ten years working at crummy jobs, writing for free, and existing on the low end of the economic spectrum in places like Providence and New York City. In that time I had kept returning to the stories in *Rock Springs*, and in the years since I have continued to do so. In Flannery O'Connor's words they "deepen the mystery," and there is always more wisdom in them—on life as well as on literature—to be gleaned. In *Rock Springs* Ford captures a peculiarly American rhythm and tone that I'm not sure a young person full of hope can understand all at once because it has to do with the experience of loss, with the "high lonesome" that is the shadow of our most cherished national myths— the responsibility inherent in our freedom, the isolation inherent in our self-awareness, the disappointment inherent in our dreams.

There is the young narrator of *Great Falls*, struggling to understand how what he thought was a happy home has just detonated in the last twenty-four hours:

Though possibly it—the answer—is simple: it is just low-life, some coldness in us all, some helplessness that causes us to misunderstand life

when it is pure and plain, makes our existence seem like a border
between two nothings, and makes us no more or less than animals who
meet on the road—watchful, unforgiving, without patience or desire.

And there is the narrator I treasure most from *Rock Springs*, Les, of "Communist." Looking back on a series of events that occurred in his last days of living at home, Les relates to the reader his realization of the price his mother paid, out of her own life, for his:

And how old was I then? Sixteen. Sixteen is young, but it can also be a
grown man. I am forty-one years old now, and I think about that time
without regret, though my mother and I never talked in that way again,
and I have not heard her voice now in a long, long time.

When I read "Communist," particularly the last movement with its unflinching remembrance of the tragedy of the young mother's life, I think of the Control of language exhibited by poets like Keats and Stevens; but I also think of "the music of the people," the greatest of American country and western and folk music—Hank Williams and Jimmie Rodgers, Alison Krauss and Dolly Parton. I think of "Red River Valley," "Shenandoah," and "Poor Wayfaring Stranger," of their folk expression (thus closest to the truth of lived experience) of lament and loneliness:

I'm going there to meet my mother
I'm going there no more to roam
I'm just going over Jordan
I'm just going over home

These words, from "Poor Wayfaring Stranger," complement in an almost unconsciously fugal fashion those last lines of "Communist":

"I have not heard her voice now in a long, long time." Ford captures and identifies in these voices and tales from the other side of the tracks what I think is the eternal source of sadness in all of us Americans—our restlessness, the way we just can't stay home: "Would you think he was anybody like you?" It is a very complex and deeply moving achievement. And the stories achieve this while creating the illusion of somebody "just talking."

Since that day at Notre Dame, and my subsequent purchase of *Rock Springs*, I have, of course, read other books that have set off something inside me and changed how I saw and felt about things— Ralph Ellison's *Invisible Man,* Octavio Paz's essays in *The Labyrinth of Solitude,* Seamus Heaney's poems in *North,* to mention three—and though it is not a book, *Unforgiven.* But no book has gotten, in quite that way, as far down inside of me as *Rock Springs,* and made me see and feel things in such a way that how I felt about myself changed. *Rock Springs* made me see that such things could be said.

JOAN BARFOOT

The Maddest Book I Read

THE GOLDEN NOTEBOOK by Doris Lessing

Back in university I had a friend who went mad. Since he was a fledgling poet, and also had a sharp, dark, alert sense of humor (surely a sign of resilient sanity?) our rowdy crowd thought little, for a time, of what we took to be a few minor eccentricities, only slightly more advanced than everyone else's.

Not until he began waking his housemates by aiming phantom rat-a-tatting machine guns at them in their beds and threatening to kill them for reasons they could not make sense of, and then escalated matters by telephoning obscenely and menacingly and repeatedly to women he felt had rejected him, did somebody call for help. Even at that, some of us considered the help offered excessive—a swift jaunt to a hospital psych ward, followed by a journey to the more ominous local psych hospital.

. . . .

Joan Barfoot has won the Books in Canada award for the country's best first novel and the Marian Engel Award for her body of work. Her ninth novel, *Critical Injuries,* was short-listed for the Trillium Award in Canada and long-listed for the Man Booker Prize in England. She lives in Ontario, Canada.

This was just a big, familiar, awkward guy. It was hard to take too seriously the undefined troubles of a sensitive, lumbering charter member of our very own lighthearted group, and so a couple of us offered to be his custodians if he were released. We held a coming-out party for him. He spoke merrily of his "happy pills," and of "living better electrically"—by which he meant shock treatments. He stripped off his clothes and pissed in the punch and roamed about looming silently over a number of politely petrified guests.

We were in way over our heads. He was drowning.

This was my first experience with real-life trouble of this sort, and evidently I managed it poorly—as, no quick learner, I would years later botch another encounter with this same beleaguered old friend.

That first time I was still very young, though, and susceptible to romantic notions of madness. Not least of these was the appeal of the suffering-creator school of artistic achievement (all those tortured poets from high school literature classes!). Also to the point, however, was the prickly, uneven relationship I'd established in adolescence with novelist Doris Lessing.

In those poets' hands, and in hers, what I had come to imagine, suppose, even believe about madness came to this: that to feel so powerfully, to see so vividly (and never mind if the visions were hard to bear)—the pure radiance of living in the world in such heightened fashion surely must be spectacular. That view was easily affordable since I seemed to have little aptitude for madness myself. What I did have was a useful vulnerability to secondhand, literary insanity—a sort of fevered contact high at the particular hands, and mind, of Lessing.

Until I hit *The Golden Notebook*, though (and promptly began rereading it for tune-up purposes every summer), Lessing and I had had, as I say, an uneven relationship. I'd dawdled and trudged through adolescence in the company of her *Children of Violence* series of novels, with no great sparks of attachment occurring. It was enough, I suppose, that I was marginally more bolstered than bored by the similarities between her protagonist (and barely veiled alter ego) Martha Quest and myself, and reasonably intrigued by our differences.

Certainly we came from different generations and far distant parts of the world. I grew up in the 1950s and '60s on a farm outside a small city in the Canadian province of Ontario, Martha a couple of decades earlier on a remote farm outpost in what then was Rhodesia, now Zimbabwe. Both of our early social and political environments were profoundly white, although my little community, as one of the farther-flung destinations of the Underground Railroad, had a sprinkling of blacks (which is not what they were called by other residents), whereas Martha/Doris's entire country was overtly and savagely racist toward its majority black population.

Martha Quest was contemptuous of her hardscrabble family, desperate to leave them behind, which she did. I was in high-hatted adolescence a little too contemptuous of my family as well, but never intended to abandon them, and did not. In her move to the "big city," Martha fell in with local communists absorbed in issues of racial injustice (despite the serious double handicap of being white and being gripped by rigidly strenuous ideology, all in all rendering them ill-equipped to foment national revolution). In my move to the "big city," I fell in with rabble-rousing student journalists (including one crazy guy) with no clear political agenda beyond stirring the many available pots of the day and drinking a good deal.

I thought Martha Quest/Doris Lessing politically naive. She would have dismissed me as foolish and wasteful. It's likely that to a point, we would both have been right.

Lessing had moved to England by the time she published her stand-alone novel *The Golden Notebook* in 1962, and a few years later

The Four-Gated City, the culmination of that Martha Quest/Children of Violence series. Her Rhodesia may have been on the other side of the world from me, but both these books entered truly foreign territory. Now she was writing about madness, and from such compelling perspectives that wherever she went from then on—a great many directions in a brave and prolific career—I became hers for life.

In *The Golden Notebook* she wrote of madness as it might be felt and perceived and suffered from the inside, and as it is judged and diagnosed and treated from the outside. What she was pursuing was the uncommon theme of breakdown—individual, social, political— as an anguished but fundamentally creative requisite for learning the true, far, hard powers of being a whole and unified human being, human society.

It was not light reading for a relatively sane and cosseted high school kid, and got no fluffier with later rereadings. It also lost none of its power, even viewed through the subsequent unhappy darkness of my college friend's tumults.

In *The Golden Notebook* blocked novelist and troubled Communist Anna Wulf, veering toward and dodging away from insanity, uses different-colored notebooks to record and explore different aspects of her life: black for Anna the writer, red for politics, yellow for stories transformed from experience, blue as a sort of diary, mainly of flailing relationships with needy or arrogant or dim-witted or desperately troubled men. Around and around Anna goes, spiraling downward, hanging on barely.

And in the end of this chaos and clutter is intended to come something whole: the golden notebook of the title.

It is an unsparing novel of unsparing ideas, filled also with passion and energy. Novels of ideas that include real emotion in their depiction—in their very concept and definition—of high intelligence, are not exactly thick on the bookshelves. And so there again,

Lessing's theme: that separation of human interests and qualities is death to the human; that unification is, or may be, salvation.

I reread *The Golden Notebook* each summer because it upset me, discombobulated me, set up every aspect of life for examination and question: ideology, cruelty, the intimacies and chasms between women and men, justice, generosity, what is large and what is imagined to be small, the human spirit and soul, writing itself, breaking down, growing whole. Literarily speaking, Lessing would, it appeared, try anything.

Of course, there's no accounting for critics. Ten years after its publication, Lessing was still complaining that just about everyone had missed her point: "The essence of the book, the organization of it, everything in it, says implicitly and explicitly that we must not divide things off, must not compartmentalise," she wrote irritably.

Instead *The Golden Notebook* had been instantly labeled a great battle cry in the war of the sexes, and Lessing was accused of—or revered for—putting into edgy words some highly volatile intergender inflammations. Ironically, considering her intentions, critics and many readers had confused a part with the whole.

To be sure, Lessing wrote all too recognizably of how a man of any country or political persuasion or economic circumstance or charm will say or do something fatuous or patronizing or presumptuous or cruel; and a woman of any country or political persuasion or economic circumstance or charm will spit back something venomous or aggrieved, or will store her rages and resentments in silence until—something happens. She portrayed this so pungently that another of my reasons for the annual *The Golden Notebook* rereading became to test the edges of my own relationships, to see how they were holding up.

Not well, it turned out. A decade or so ago I canceled the exercise for a few years, on the grounds that living even briefly inside the novel had once again made me so restless and raw—and so viciously alert to the poor man who was trying to share parts of my life, but who had not shared the book and so, more than usually, did not grasp what was going on—that my choice came down to him or *The Golden Notebook*. And like the typically yearning-for-love female of a Lessing novel, I gave up the book—what charades we play, what lengths we will go to! Doris Lessing—or Anna Wulf, or Martha Quest—would have recognized me so clearly they might have nodded if we'd met on the street.

Now the fellow is gone, and I'm back. I'm reading *The Golden Notebook* again, and I'm thinking not of the-man-who-didn't-work-out-never-mind-what-I-stopped-reading, but of the university pal who, as they say, lost his mind.

That's not what happens, though. Minds don't get "lost"; although they may well change their shapes, become less recognizable.

After some long stretches inside various psychiatric hospitals and some much shorter stretches outside, that man, by now well into his thirties, found himself in the city where I then lived, without a place to sleep. "Come in," I said, "Of course you can stay in my house." He had a diagnosis, he announced rather proudly. He was officially "manic-depressive." The naming of his illness, although it scarcely seemed to me to encompass his troubles, gave it a legitimacy and solidity it lacked when it was something unnamed and mysterious that leaped on him out of the darkness, and he found this a comfort.

He was very angry, though, if in a soft-spoken, highly medicated sort of way. We sat at my pine kitchen table as he talked of conspiracies against him. Some of these dated back to events I'd witnessed and people I knew, and who I knew had not been his enemies. He saw every particle of existence entirely from his own perspective—an extreme, well-gnarled instance of a most common human affliction. I believed his versions were mainly off-key, off-kilter, but was helpless to correct them. And moreover, as we sat at that kitchen table hour after hour, then day after day, I felt myself being drawn in, further and further, to what he was seeing, the convoluted ways that he saw. I understood more and more clearly how he had come to the conclusions he had. I could also see that this was dangerous, that it might be easy to begin with a welcoming mind that slipped into an open mind, and wound up a badly distorted one.

It was interesting to me that this experience was not unlike reading *The Golden Notebook* into whose explorations and experiences of madness I was also capable of falling—deliberately, though, not like this, with a real tortured man going on and on in my kitchen, lonely and wanting company inside his torment.

I continued to suppose, right along with Lessing, that becoming whole, in every sense she cared to name, might well be preceded by breaking everything down. I also thought, though, that this sort of breakdown and recovery into wholeness was too rare and too brave for most of us—almost certainly too brave for me, which is why I read her rather than peering too directly at whatever insanities of my own might be lurking. And then, too, what was there to say of madness that came not from strain and battle and determination and despair and muddle and even hallucination and dream, but from such arbitrary missteps as out-of-whack chemicals?

Lessing might reply, who is to say what is out of whack? Madness, after all, can just be something judged odd and inconvenient by those who can stand back and punish behavior that doesn't match some relatively arbitrary convention.

True enough, I would say, but what of madness that causes awful actual harm; or that assaults someone who cannot fight back? Lessing's women and men are never really beyond fighting back. Or, by acquiescing to and examining their own insanity, finally making their way through it. This is wonderfully hopeful.

My old comrade was different. If at some point in his illness he could have worked through it to save and redeem himself, by the time he was spinning tales of conspiracy and ill will at my kitchen table, the possibility had been thoroughly blasted. That may have been because of those earlier shock treatments, years of major medication, or some tilt in his own chemistries, but he surely wasn't headed in any of the directions Lessing's characters achieved. He was skidding, and the seductive notion that pain spoken and shared might be either worked with or halved was clearly wrong. Pain spoken and shared in my kitchen was becoming contagious.

And so here is the flat, true, brutal ending: I pulled away, I made him leave my home, I saved myself. I was very grateful for those useful, interesting, extraordinary days, and enormously relieved to end them. Rereading *The Golden Notebook* (or *The Four-Gated City,* either will do), and lapsing again into the raw-skinned, hyper-alert, and blessedly temporary strange state that results, brings me as close to insanity as I'm currently willing to get. I continue to believe that humans' habit of splitting ourselves into sections, dividing the parts of our lives from each other part, is a kind of original sin, leading us into practically all our human disasters. I realize that from the Lessing perspective, and even my own, I am nevertheless probably busy most of the time "blocking" some whole and splendid potential in favor of getting on, best I can, with what passes for regular life.

I am also more than old enough to know that even brave, wise, magnificent novels cannot be, should not be, are not intended to be, recipe books. I don't know what happened to my old friend, and I have not tried to find out.

MARIANNE GINGHER

The Most Double-D-Daring Book I Read
THE ROBBER BRIDEGROOM by Eudora Welty

I have read many splendid tributes to Eudora Welty since her death. Her devoted friends and admirers praise her genius and grace and generosity and have commented that, throughout her life, she maintained a childlike sense of wonder. It's this latter quality with which I identify. It's a quality that consistently informed her fiction with the wit of the prankster, a love of the far-fetched, the wide-eyed observations of someone who, throughout her life, turned common detail into marvel. I've never read Eudora Welty without being reminded of what made me love reading as a child: the sense of wow.

The books I loved growing up were the ones that combined drollery and mischief with the sort of close-call daring that a kid yearned to imitate. *The Five Chinese Brothers* by

. . . .

Marianne Gingher is the author of four books, including the novel *Bobby Rex's Greatest Hit* and her memoir, *A Girl's Life: Horses, Boys, Weddings & Luck*. She teaches at the University of North Carolina at Chapel Hill.

Claire Hutchet Bishop was such a book, and the kids at Sternberger Elementary School in Greensboro, North Carolina, competed to check it out and swagger proudly around, brandishing it like pirate's loot. That book had clout, largely due to the fact that it was a story about getting away with murder—something all kids hanker to know about in their wee little underdog souls. The book's slippery ethics provoked rather than coddled, and the story was just disturbing enough to satisfy a child's desire to know something about the waffling nature of truth that adults weren't yet ready to divulge. I experienced the same sort of jolt reading it that I got whenever I double-d-dared myself to thumb through my father's medical textbooks, braving the photographs of people with advanced cases of exotic and disfiguring diseases.

As I grew up and my reading tastes broadened, I still delighted in the knowledge apprehended in childhood that some books reverberated like gongs or sirens or trumpet calls to action. They ignited fuses, ripped rugs out from under us, were like thumbtacks planted in our chairs or Whoopee Cushions. No book that mattered deeply to me fostered meekness. I reacted to certain books in the same way I reacted to dares. They disappeared all notions of feeling ordinary or docile or well behaved, and I became a bolder person after I had read some of them. Books have emboldened me to argue with friends, to fall deeply in love and stay that way, to be kinder to strangers, to stick up for myself and, once, to crash a party in order to meet my literary hero.

It was gentle Eudora Welty's rowdy little romance, *The Robber Bridegroom*, that incited me to throw protocol and every good manner my mother ever taught me out the window and barge my way into a party, uninvited. I blame that book entirely with its spitfire heroine, its rollicking blend of American folklore, European fairy tale, and confection of language so luscious I wanted to eat every page. Best of all, *The Robber Bridegroom* was written in 1942, when political correctness was only a tyrannical gleam in the critic's eye. Just imagine! A writer could write about a bandit who kidnapped a plantation owner's daughter, deflowered her (the maid enjoyed it!), and set her up cooking and cleaning for him and his band of rogues in an isolated hovel. Not only does she not complain, she whistles like a lark while she love-slaves her life away.

Welty's only thematic agenda was to weave a sly and witty entertainment, wicked with hyperbole, that portrays the profound gains and losses inherent in civilizing a behemoth Southern wilderness. This is a madcap bucking bronco of a book filled with galloping diversions that have confounded and irritated literary scholars looking to rein it in. That must be the chief reason it enthralled me.

I came upon it at a time in my education when I relished the refreshment of literature that reminded me of why I had loved reading as a child—for the sensation of wholehearted adventure.

I didn't read Eudora Welty until the early 1970s, when I was in graduate school. Somehow, although I had grown up in the South, I had missed all the Southern writers, except Faulkner. Not all of Welty's fiction is as fanciful as *The Robber Bridegroom,* of course, but the chief appeal to me of all her writing is its Yeats-like lyricism and imagery as concrete and well aimed as a stone expertly skipped across water. I thought of myself in those days as a failed poet. That Welty, a writer of fiction, could transform the drudge and drone of prose into language as airborne as birdsong seemed nothing short of miraculous to me—and an inspiration.

My teacher, Fred Chappell, frequently suggested books I might enjoy, recommending everything from Aristotle to Tolstoy to H. P. Lovecraft. On one occasion we were standing near a bookshelf in his den, and something I had said made him reach for *The Robber Bridegroom.*

"You ever read this?" he asked. "Here. Take it. It's a dandy."

He handed me the glowing little book, a plain-covered war-issue first edition published by Harcourt Brace. Chappell himself admired Welty's work, knew her personally, and more than once, as we hunched over beers after class at the fabulous Pickwick bar on Walker Avenue in Greensboro, he had drummed up interest among Welty fans for a road trip down to Jackson, Mississippi, to call on her. "But what would she say to a bunch of student scalawags busting in on her like that?" one of us scalawags asked.

"Miss Eudora, she'd be proud to meet us," Fred assured us. "She'd say, 'Come on in, y'all, and eat a bite of my marble cake.' "

We never got around to taking that road trip, but we romanticized it into breathtaking possibility. And the fact that Fred knew Welty and spoke of her in familiar and endearing terms, humanized her, set a twinkle in her otherwise purely visionary eye, and seemed to narrow the great divide between our discipleship and her stature as literary icon. For some reason, young writers need to believe that the authors of the books they esteem have real lives apart from the pages they write. That they might actually know how to bake a marble cake and be gracious to scalawags was a spectacular gleaning.

I took *The Robber Bridegroom* home and gulped it down in one sitting, admiring its mix of beauty and rambunctiousness. On a second reading I paid close attention to the many liberties Welty takes with the conventions of the tale. Her heroine, Rosamond, is no passive fairy tale princess waiting for some prince to rouse her from her stupor with a kiss. Rosamond is spirited, industrious, and loyal; but she is also habituated to lying and takes a few pratfalls normally reserved for the buffoon. The book's hero, Jamie Lockhart, thief and lover, is no paragon of family values. He is, however, a hero "with the power to look both ways and see a thing from all sides." Sometimes his hesitation and thoughtfulness waylay his success. It's the couple's lack of perfection, their rascally virtue that defines Jamie and Rosamond as recognizably modern.

My third reading of the book was a submersion in language. I found myself trying to memorize passages I admired so that when I returned the book—which was then out of print—the afterglow of its imagery would permanently flicker across my brain. I read of one character so festooned with jewelry "that she gave out spangles the way a porcupine gives out quills." A bucket of fresh milk had "the sound of foam in it." Daylight was so tentative "that the green was first there, then not there in the treetops, but green seemed to beat on the air like a pulse." Six ugly girls were "as weighted down with freckles as a fig tree is with figs."

Several months passed before I felt ready to part with the book. To tell the truth, my brain felt feverish from reading it so many times, a little wild and woolly. When Fred opened the door, I'm sure I looked like somebody who needed to have her temperature taken. I apologized for the late return. "How'd you like it?" he asked.

"It's one of the most unruly books I ever read," I declared.

Fred laughed. As he took the book, I imagined he could feel its palpitations in sync with my own.

"Romance, murder, sorrow, comedy, violence, charm, and poetry—it has everything. I loved it so much I've been trying to memorize it."

"Here," Fred said, and handed the book back to me. "You keep it then."

The surprise and gratitude I felt bordered on delirium, but I pushed the little book right back at him.

"No," he said. "Since you loved it that much, it now belongs to you."

"But I can't."

"And why's that?"

"Because I almost stole it from you anyway!"

"Pshaw!" Fred said. He really did use that word—and with genuine spluttering dismay.

"But it's a first edition of a rare book that's out of print. How could you bear to give it away?"

He looked amused, and with one index finger, he tapped his forehead. "Because I've got it up here," he said, "and here," he said, touching his heart. And that was that.

Years later, when I was teaching as an adjunct at a college that will go unnamed, Miss Eudora Welty, her very own self, was invited to receive a special honor, and the buzz went out in the English department that there was to be a party to celebrate her visit. Of course I laid out my most glamorous dress and shined my shoes and waited for my invitation. It was no oversight that an invitation never arrived. I heard through the poison ivy vine that only tenured writing faculty had been invited to the party along with assorted dignitaries and representatives from a certain Southern Lit mafia and other ruling elite. There were some folks going who didn't know her work at all and thought Eudora Welty—like Betty Crocker—was a brand of marble cake mix.

A colleague of mine, also an uninvited adjunct but with friends in high places, happened one day to run into the woman who was hosting the gala. The English department had issued the invitations and when the hostess discovered that my colleague hadn't been sent one, she invited her to come on the spot.

Immediately my friend called me up. "You're coming with me. We'll dress up like a couple of haunts and spook everybody," she schemed. And it did seem to me that some vengeful trickery was called for. I felt the kind of smoldering agitation in my bones that had motivated even mild-mannered characters in *The Robber Bridegroom* to risk their reputations in certain acts of aggression.

Rosamond and Jamie were always showing up places uninvited. I imagined the faces of guests at the party registering shock and indignation as I whooshed my way past them on my determined pilgrimage to meet my literary hero.

It was a big deal to crash this sort of party. Besides the breach in etiquette, the blow to my dignity, the possibility of my hero's icy reception, the heightened sense of feeling marginalized (an interloping fan turned beggarly, discourteous clodhopper), I thought my job was at stake. What I think I feared most was the validated scorn of certain power brokers in the English department. Back then, at that particular institution, folks who taught creative writing were already suspect as upstarts and pretenders, rather than scholars, and they suffered a status somewhere between cockroach and mule. It was possible that when my name came up for reappointment, I'd be reassessed as a troublemaker, a pest, and the professors' meeting room would buzz with dismissive remarks. "Call Orkin," I imagined someone saying.

On the evening of the party, my adjunct friend and I stole effortlessly inside that enchanted place where nobody seemed to notice our trespass. Welty's presence had cast a gentling spell over all. The chairman of the English department didn't flinch at our arrival. He beamed at me and inquired after my well-being. Not a single guest noticed the little horns that had burst through the skin of my forehead or my cloven feet galumphing along in my strappy dress-up sandals. It felt as if I'd entered some dreamy chapter of *The Robber Bridegroom* itself where the worst situation transformed magically into best.

There, on a sofa, in a shiny mint blue taffeta dress, Miss Welty sat unengaged.

Like the jostling rings in orbit around a splash, guests circled her with plates of food and glasses of champagne. She was just sitting there, a regular person, waiting to have someone to talk to. Her gifted hands lay idle in her lap. The flourish of luminous curls upon her brow made her seem less imposingly monolithic, and more like a Corinthian column at ease.

There was, too, something mischievous in her expression, some quality of playfulness and curiosity that I had always associated with her writing. Her face conveyed an expansive tolerance that had served her well as she had cackled and crooned, wept and cheered, grimaced, gloated, guffawed, and swooned over every utterance, thought, and deed that she had attributed to her characters. I imagined that I saw, in the calm pond of her face, Jamie Lockhart and Rosamond Musgrove, double-d-daring me to introduce myself.

In her autobiographical *One Writer's Beginnings,* Welty writes that "all serious daring starts from within." She doesn't mean, however, that inward daring grows in a vacuum. It's not something our hearts make up from scratch. It begins as an inkling of self-expansion, sparked by something outside ourselves: a riff of spellbinding music, a beckoning landscape, the roar of an unforgettable sunset— or a book. Inspiration is the genesis of most dares.

I was received by Miss Welty with genteel courtesy. I sat down on the sofa beside her and gained her rapt attention until some other party guest commanded it away.

I felt a bit like Rosamond, whose predicament had at first seemed woeful but who enjoyed spectacular triumph by novel's end. I had ample time to thank Miss Welty for the bold experiment in whimsy that *The Robber Bridegroom* lets loose and to tell her how, even at that moment as I sat speaking with her, I felt its intrepid influence. As concrete proof, I dipped a hand into my purse and produced my lovely copy of the book that Fred Chappell had given me, and I told Miss Welty that story, which she enjoyed. Then in my most gauche but emboldened moment of the evening, I, the party crasher, the troll that might have crawled out of that book's very pages to sit beside its author, asked Miss Welty to autograph *The Robber Bridegroom,* and she obliged. I believe she would have welcomed a bona fide troll just as happily, and, smiling a conspiratorial smile, signed its book with glee.

J. PEDER ZANE

The Hippest Book I Read

CIVILIZATION AND ITS DISCONTENTS by Sigmund Freud

Like most American teenagers, I wanted to be hip. With it. On the edge. Rebels, after all, were the most popular dudes around.

I listened to the right music, wore the right clothes, and went to every party. I said "man." A lot. I saw myself as an outlaw, a crazy, roistering wild man who broke all the rules.

Then I encountered Sigmund Freud.

It was my senior year in college, and I knew big change was coming; perhaps that is why his life and work had such a strong effect on me. He was a dead genius, and I was a questioning kid, but still I saw deep similarities. Like me, Freud grew up in a loving home and went to good schools. He was a hard worker who married and reared a family in middle-class com-

. . . .

J. Peder Zane is the book review editor of the *News & Observer* of Raleigh, North Carolina. His weekly column has received numerous national honors including the Distinguished Writing Award for Commentary from the American Society of Newspaper Editors.

fort. The same things, I had to admit, that I wanted for myself. On the surface he was bourgeois to the max, the very opposite of hip.

But as I read *Civilization and Its Discontents* (1930), he also seemed the hippest guy on the street. It was the wildest, most audacious, out-there, kick-butt book I had ever read. It crackled with risk-taking creativity. This dour man in a jacket and tie was a subversive of heroic courage, who gave free rein to thoughts that challenged the very foundations of society.

What a combination.

In this short work (my copy of the standard edition translated by James Strachey runs just 104 pages), Freud offers radical insights into the nature of beauty, love, and the sources of religion. In his more far-flung moments, he discusses our complicated relations with dogs, how man's upright gait provoked feelings of shame, the changing meaning of the menstrual cycle in sexual relations, and why houses are substitutes "for the mother's womb."

But those are only side trips in Freud's mind-bending journey. In prose as controlled as a surgeon's scalpel but as free as a dancer's leap—God, I wish I could write like that—he tackles the central question of life. But instead of wondering, "How can I be happy?" he asks, "Why is it so hard to be happy?"

To my young mind, Freud's dark twist on this age-old riddle was hipness personified. Mocking the feel-good philosophies society peddles, it seemed a revelation of hidden truth. My phoniness meter was finely tuned back then (thanks, Holden), so I was enthralled when Freud began answering his question by exposing a fundamental hypocrisy: People say they follow Jesus' call to "love your neighbor as yourself" but, Freud argues, the Roman playwright Plautus described our more familiar conduct: "Man is a wolf to man."

For Freud, this inescapable conflict between love and hate, between reason and instinct, is the dynamic force of each individual's life and the history of our species. In a tour de force of scientific insight and poetic imagination—God, I wish I could think like that—he attributes this struggle to two great instincts. Eros, the life instinct, urges us to fall in love, to cooperate with our fellow man, to build great societies. Eros gives wings to our better angels.

Problem is, we also have a "death instinct," a devilish reservoir of our inherent aggression, of our desire to destroy rather than create, which opposes the whole lovely scheme:

Men are not gentle creatures who want to be loved . . . their neighbor is for them not only a potential helper or sexual object, but also someone who tempts them to satisfy their aggressiveness on him, to exploit his capacity for work without compensation, to use him sexually without his consent, to seize his possessions, to humiliate him, to cause him pain, to torture and to kill him.

Civilization, then, is a mass insurance policy against the death instinct. Its terms boil down to this: "Don't clobber me and I won't clobber you. If you do, the group will punish you." It establishes laws and mores, setting out what is permitted and what is proscribed, allowing Eros to flourish.

Unfortunately, while we might agree that society serves our larger self-interest, we chafe at its restrictions: It frustrates our desires and leaves us with pools of aggression that we are not allowed to satisfy.

As a young man I knew all about pent-up anger and frustration. Reading Freud, it—I—suddenly made sense. He gave me a feeling of self-knowledge I'd never known before. Now I knew the score. I was in control. But then the old hipster laid one more unsettling truth on me.

Society, Freud says, does not trust us to handle our frustrated impulses. So it has devised an ingenious, though discomfiting, way to hurl that aggressiveness we would like to exercise upon others back on ourselves. It accomplishes this through the Superego—which Freud posits as the third territory of the mind, along with that home of our wildest passions, the Id, and the Ego, which seeks to mediate the claims of its combative brain-mates.

The Superego performs a sort of cultural alchemy: It transforms the aggression that threatens civilization into pacifying psychic states that serve it, our conscience and sense of guilt. Part of our mind, the Superego knows our every secret. It is a cop who never goes off duty. It need not catch us in the act but pounces at the mere hatching of a plan. "Bad intentions are equated with bad actions, and hence comes a need for punishment and a sense of guilt." Few men, for example, actually kill their fathers and sleep with their mothers. But, according to Freud, they all want to. Instead of congratulating us for renouncing these Oedipal wishes, the Superego swats us for simply harboring them. The fact these desires are instinctual and, often unconscious, matters not a whit to it. We feel stricken, but don't know why.

It gets worse.

With each new collar, the Superego becomes empowered and emboldened. "Every renunciation of instinct now becomes a dynamic source of conscience and every fresh renunciation increases [its] severity and intolerance." Thus, Freud argues, the more virtuous we are, the guiltier we feel. For those who routinely tell their Superegos to buzz off, society builds jails and asylums (and artist's colonies).

Damned if we do, damned if we don't. Abandon civilization, and we better sleep with one eye open. Embrace it, and we must hand the reins over to our own personal Officer Krupke. "What we call civilization," Freud concludes, "is largely responsible for our misery."

Terrific.

When I first read *Civilization and Its Discontents,* I found Freud's pessimism deeply appealing. When we're children, our elders try to give us a rosy view of the world—every Christmas a jolly guy we've never met gives us presents! By our teen years, it become clear that there's another, more troubling side, to the story. "Aha!" we say, "so that's the real deal."

We become angry at the manipulation, at being made the fool. No wonder the hippest kids embrace the darkest visions. What *Civilization and Its Discontents* said to me was: "Look at what is being done to you."

As I've gotten older, I've become more hopeful and less smitten with Freud's views. Yes, there are people who feel miserable, and, yes, Hitler and history's other monsters have revealed the savage potential that exists in us all. But most people are far less conflicted, guilty, and unhappy than Freud allows. Our nasty urges are far less powerful than he assumes. Eros, the death instinct,and the Superego may be playing their parts in each of us at this very moment, but the result is not discontent. It is a wide range of changing feelings in people leading generally satisfying lives. Could we be happier? Sure. Are we perpetually miserable? I don't think so.

However, those reservations are of little importance. It is not Freud's conclusions but his approach, an unsurpassed model of daring, conviction, and originality, that still inspires me. Fearless, freewheeling, and iconoclastic, it embodies the very essence of hipness. Freud showed me that hipness isn't about buying, wearing, or believing the right things—those who glom onto such accouterments are, ironically, simply advertising their conventionality. It's a mind-set that questions everything not because rebellion is cool but because that is the only way to clear your own path. I had sought hipness as a means of belonging; Freud taught me that it is really about going it alone.

Hipness isn't about keeping up, but keeping on. It's a chimera, like the rainbow's end, a destination that is useful precisely because it can never be reached. The minute you think you're there, you've stopped felling the trees and cutting the brush.

HAVEN KIMMEL

The Most Familiar Book I Read

SOUTH OF THE BIG FOUR by Don Kurtz

Of that famous Midwestern novel, Robert James Waller's *The Bridges of Madison County*, my friend James provided my favorite assessment: "Every word in it is a lie." I'd been wrangling with that book in my head for years, and James's assessment was comforting. So the book sold millions of copies while ignoring all the conventions of the novel, i.e., plot, characterization, verisimilitude? So Waller perpetuated a sentimental hoax that was taken seriously by countless women—that it is morally correct, indeed it is the idyllic option, to stay in the lonely farmhouse and serve your family rather than to live an even remotely fulfilling life? And so the male protagonist was a transparent attempt to sell Waller himself to the world as a sensitive, folk-singing, kitchen-dancing Alpha male? It was all a lie.

. . . .

Haven Kimmel is the author of four books, the memoir *A Girl Named Zippy*, a children's book, *Orville: A Dog Story*, and two novels, *The Solace of Leaving Early* and *Something Rising (Light and Swift)*. She lives in Durham, North Carolina.

But more treacherous than Waller's crimes against aesthetics was that the public took *Bridges* seriously as a novel of the Midwest. He romanticized that part of the country without giving so much as a sentence to the truth of the place. I had long despaired of the world ever seeing my postage stamp of native soil as anything but a breeding ground for wall-eyed reactionaries, and here was a person who wound up with access to lots and lots of readers and had constructed the opposite falsification: a rural dreamscape dotted with covered bridges, Italian women sitting on porches waiting for their children to get home from a picturesque 4-H fair. In truth, covered bridges get torn down because they can't be used by farmers, or they're set ablaze by pot-smoking juvenile delinquents. They're just dry, old tinder, after all. And Francesca, the voluptuous Italian housewife living in Iowa? Oh yeah, that happens. This isn't to say that my very own home state of Indiana hasn't produced writers who've been telling the truth all along, among them Jessamyn West, Scott Russell Sanders, and Michael Martone. But generally Hoosier writers don't reach a wide-enough audience, or if they do, as in the case of Kurt Vonnegut, they're not writing about Indiana at all. There are undoubtedly good reasons for this.

In 1995 I moved from Indiana to Chapel Hill, North Carolina, leaving behind old friends and familiar roads, for a college town that was part Southern, part a retirement home for wealthy Yankees, where no one knew me and hardly anyone was friendly. I spent much of that first Southern summer in the library, immersing myself in the works of some of North Carolina's best contemporary writers, including Lee Smith and Alan Gurganus, Clyde Edgerton, Lawrence Naumoff, and Reynolds Price. I was trying to understand my new home—I made a real effort—but found myself near tears every time I heard Garrison Keillor's voice (a bad sign), every time I saw an advertisement for pesticides. There are those who will mock: I missed Indiana?! And not the pretty part of it, but east-central and northern Indiana, the part people imagine as the portal to Death? All I can say is the heart has its ways. Millions of people choose to live in Los Angeles. We love what's familiar, what has been imprinted on us. For me the landscape of the imagination is flat and wide and the horizon never changes; there are no mountains, no water, no Starbucks, only land where you can run and run for miles. No one ever agrees with me on this point, the harsh beauty of the place. Imagine my surprise, then, the day I found Don Kurtz's novel, *South of the Big Four,* on the new-release shelf at the library. I'd never heard of Kurtz, but one look at the cover was enough for me: a wide white border, and a beautiful blue and sepia-toned photograph of a field and sky, just earth, with a stand of trees at the vanishing point. I checked it out without reading the jacket copy, because that phrase, "the Big Four," could have come from only one place. Home.

South of the Big Four is the story of Arthur Conasen, who returns to the farmland of northern Indiana after years of working on ore boats on the Great Lakes. In other parts of the world, if you name your protagonist Arthur, the reader can expect something grand. A kingdom at stake. This Arthur's Camelot is a cold, abandoned farmhouse at the edge of a difficult piece of land. The house was formerly owned by Arthur's widowed father, who raised three sons there (and lost one in a farm accident), then lost the house and land to a younger man, who would eventually lose it to another. Everything, from the Prologue on, is pitch perfect. "I do remember old Si Lemke in that Vo-Ag class now and then, reciting for us the rule the bankers always followed: don't make any farm loans south of the Big Four Railroad. After all the good things have been taken, there are others still in line—for my family that meant a share of that same swampy land south of the tracks no one else had wanted." The novel opens with a lesson in economics, and rightly so. In Indiana, a farm is an *operation*, not a stab at authenticity, and where there are operations there are necessarily bankers. Where there are bankers there's a constant undercurrent of danger and treachery: the same man who is glad-handing you today will sell the farm out from under you tomorrow.

Kurtz made three brilliant narrative decisions. He tells the story in the first person, in a flat, taciturn voice; not an easy task, as Arthur has to reveal the entire drama, which is both moving and profound, without any emotion of his own. Kurtz places Arthur on the outlaw end of the Midwestern social continuum—he's the last born, he left home long ago, he's unmarried, and he cares nothing about the conventions of polite society. In other words, Arthur is on one side of the Big Four and everyone with power and property is on the other, including his brother Byron, now the vice principal of Tippy Valley high school. (For the record, my high school was called Blue River Valley, and, of course, a Byron-type was our assistant principal, because to be the principal or the superintendent would suggest a sort of success the sons of a poor farmer can't ever quite achieve.) Byron is perfectly drawn, all the way down to the painful geometry of his new ranch house, the irrevocable softening of his masculinity (the result of going from farm boy to administrator), his painful, but entirely respectable, marriage to Kendra—a good farm wife with two small children and an unfortunately strong interest in Arthur. There's a world there, and quite a fine novel: the lost parents, the lost farm, the dead brother. Yet after only a few pages Kurtz delivers his masterstroke in the form of Gerry Maars. He's the man with the biggest stake in the county, the man who, in fact, took a good deal of Arthur's family's land away from them and added it to his already vast empire. Gerry invites Arthur to work as a full-time farmhand for him, and again, everything you need to know about the Midwest is in the gesture: letting bygones go, the importance of getting the crop in on time, the shades of competition between inarticulate men. The book shifts, then, to tell the story of Arthur and Gerry.

Growing up I knew at least one person exactly like each character in this book, but Gerry Maars is the most familiar of all. In fact, there was someone in my extended family like him, a man I'll call Frank. Frank, like Gerry, was both a farmer and a businessman and held public office, and to both men that combination seemed the height a person could reach. Gerry Maars is a hail, bluff, big man with big machines who wants to get his mind around things; he's a thinker, in his way. And he can see where life goes astray, the places he's failed as a husband and father, the ways other people might resent him for the sheer bulk of his life. Frank, too, was a physically imposing man who attended church and who modeled his life on certain philosophical precepts, all the while gaining success in business with livestock and on the county council. But ultimately, both men, the fictional and the real, were concerned with one thing: power. And what is that, in a state the rest of the country completely overlooks? If we say someone in New York is powerful, we probably mean on the world's stage, but in Indiana power is entirely local. Kurtz masters this with one deft detail after another. Gerry, for instance, owns cases of soda he bought during a cheerleading fund-raiser. It's stacked in his garage next to an assortment of unused sporting equipment. (When I was growing up, having a *garage* was exotic. Soda was out of the question.) Gerry stops for breakfast every morning in a local diner and picks up the check on every table he passes. He drives a Fleetwood, and when not actually farming, usually wears a dress-up windbreaker. All of these things were true of Frank, too, down to the make of the car. And for both men, the most important question in life, the one that kept them awake at night, was not what kind of husbands and fathers they were, or even what kind of farmers, but how to maintain their tenuous grip on rural riches.

When I read the book the first time, that initial summer in Chapel Hill, I was so struck by the accuracy of the details (he calls Indiana "a state chockful of grudges") that I started to make note of the more salient ones in a journal. After a few chapters I had to stop, because I realized that in many ways the book *is* the details, and Kurtz is such a good writer that they flow past like a breeze. (I imagine that only people who grew up on farms or ranches might be moved to tears by the image of the dusty mirror Gerry Maars keeps tacked up to the side of a horse stall in his barn, a three-legged stool in front of it, for straightening himself up between combining and council meetings.) But when I reread it a few months ago, the book was brand new to me. It's been almost eight years since the novel was released; eight years ago I had lived the story one way, and now I've lived it another.

Eight years ago I didn't feel a flutter of panic when Gerry casually mentioned to Arthur that the local bank had been sold to a corporation. And when Gerry's checks began to bounce, I took it as a fact of life in a volatile business. The first time I read the novel, I saw change as simply that, but this time I knew that Kurtz had quite elegantly buried the most sinister force in a man's life, buried it in the frantic day-to-day of trying to get more than a thousand acres planted before a storm. Gerry tells a joke in the diner one morning, for example, an old Indiana warhorse of a joke, about an uncontrollably randy rooster. Eight years ago I laughed, remembering my best friend from childhood, the little red-haired Julie Newman, telling me the same joke as we lay on her bed, the Newman's farmland stretched out all around us. But this time, when Gerry Maars got to the punchline and held his finger up to the sky, pointing to the circling buzzards, I saw what Kurtz had intended all along.

Frank, my own personal Gerry Maars, picked up the checks and won the elections, stacked the cases of treasure in his garage. He must have heard that same joke countless times. And then the bank changed hands, and his checks began to bounce, and younger men came in and took his business and his land. It's hard to describe how *slick* that road is to anyone who hasn't been on it, the road that goes straight down. Or the way the men who had admired and respected Frank when he was the landed gentry took such pains to humiliate him later. Those humiliations are subtle, but they register as a catastrophe, the way a mechanic wouldn't work on a machine Frank had to have that minute, his life and livelihood up against the clock. The way he ended up working *for* the smarmy young men who'd stolen his business. His skin turned gray, he was suddenly too tired to watch a basketball game, he checked into a hospital and was dead five days later. We buried him less than a year ago.

In many ways the story of Arthur Conasen is an old one: a prodigal son returns home, only to discover that everything he left behind is long gone. The war between brothers: we know how that goes. And even Arthur's sad relationships with women, where all the sweetness is in what's left out and unsaid, are recognizable to anyone who's known a man who works with his hands and his back. But that sharp, exhausted love between Arthur and Gerry Maars, the brutal hours they toil together against the rising doom, that's a story that I've never seen told so convincingly, or with such compassion. The beauty and bleakness of the novel are the perfect objective correlative for the Indiana landscape I knew. I still haven't figured out much about the New South, as long as I've been here, but I know the land South of the Big Four Railroad, and I can say one thing with certainty: Even without a gorgeous Italian housewife, every word of Don Kurtz's heartbreaking book is true.

H. W. BRANDS

The Most Incomprehensible Book I Read

THE EDUCATION OF HENRY ADAMS by Henry Adams

I met Henry Adams when I was eighteen and he was almost seventy. He would have been still older—much older—had he not suspended the aging process by writing a memoir that, in essence, froze his world in 1907. As it was, he lived too long: He never forgave the twentieth century for not being the eighteenth, an era far more congenial to his temper and tastes.

So there was this gulf of generations between us. And it didn't grow any smaller upon my reading—or trying to read—*The Education of Henry Adams*. Was I wholly at fault in expecting a book with such a title to deal with the early years of Mr. Adams? It did, but only in the most elliptical fashion. To begin with, there was his puzzling third-person approach. The sum of my exposure to American memoirs at that point might have

. . . .

H. W. Brands is Distinguished Professor of History at Texas A&M University. He has written sixteen books, including *T.R.: The Last Romantic*, *The Age of Gold: The California Gold Rush and the New American Dream*, and *The First American: The Life and Times of Benjamin Franklin*, which was a finalist for the Pulitzer Prize.

included one or two books beyond *The Autobiography of Benjamin Franklin,* but I can't recall what they were. Franklin's style was as plain as a Quaker meetinghouse (I would learn what subtleties plainness can hide, but not till later). Adams's prose was quite the opposite. "Had he been born in Jerusalem," he wrote on the first page:

under the shadow of the Temple and circumcised in the Synagogue by his uncle the high priest, under the name of Israel Cohen, he would scarcely have been more distinctly branded, and not much more heavily handicapped in the races of the coming century, in running for such stakes as the century was to offer; but, on the other hand, the ordinary traveler, who does not enter the field of racing, finds advantages in being, so to speak, ticketed through life, with the safeguards of an old, established traffic.

Things didn't get any easier after that. The author (Adams or Cohen or whoever) spoke of places as people, for reasons that were never quite clear: Quincy (Massachusetts, I gathered) did so and so, State Street (in Boston) did such and such. The chapter titles—"Vis Inertiae," "Vis Nova," "Nunc Age," "Teufelsdrockh"—were road signs in a country that lacked English. Large parts of the book read like an obscure physics text, describing life in terms of horsepower, degrees centigrade, and ratios of volume to heat.

What was especially puzzling, and frustrating to a college freshman, was to hear my instructor refer to the book—over and over again—as one of the great works of American literature. The course was listed as "American Intellectual History" and had been recommended to me by an upperclassman of my acquaintance. Not knowing one kind of history from another, I naively enrolled—only to discover that what I had thought would be a history of the American intellect (whatever that might have been) was instead a history of

American intellectuals. Henry Adams wasn't the most impenetrable of the bunch; Charles Peirce probably took that prize. But Adams was the one of whom the instructor was the most enamored, and hence the one—when I found his autobiography so opaque—who made me feel the most like an idiot, or at least an utter unsophisticate.

For reasons now lost, I didn't get rid of my copy of the book at the end of the semester. I'd like to think that something in me responded to the challenge of Adams (or perhaps of the instructor), that some small voice told me to try him again when I had more leisure or life experience. Maybe that was it, or maybe I complained so loudly about the course that no one in my dorm wanted to enroll in it, leaving me with no takers for the texts. But the result was that Henry Adams followed me around for the next several years, from dorm to apartment to house, perched accusingly on my bookshelf. I eventually got a job as a traveling salesman, and with hours to kill in Motel 6s across the American West, I decided to renew our acquaintance.

As a person who is now both a writer and a teacher, I have become acutely aware that while all of Caesar's Gaul may be divided into three parts, all of literature divides into two—two parts against which the customary categories of prose and poetry, fiction and non-fiction pale into insignificance. These fundamental categories are the required and the discretionary. The former category includes books assigned for classes, contracted to reviewers, or containing information essential to particular readers; the latter category encompasses everything read for pleasure or casual edification. While works in the required category should be short and clear, those in the discretionary category can be as long winded and discursive as the author wants, as long as they hold the reader's attention. (As I have argued to editors when writing books intended for the second category, if a book is good at three hundred pages, it can be twice as good at six hundred pages. They haven't always been convinced—perhaps partly because every book they edit falls, by virtue of the fact that they are editing it, into their required-reading category.)

Obviously, what is required reading for one person can be discretionary reading for another; and what is required reading for one person at one time can be discretionary at another time. So it was that when Henry and I were reintroduced, somewhere in Nevada or Wyoming in the winter of 1976, our relationship took an entirely new turn. There was no longer any voice of authority telling me that this was great literature and Henry Adams the American Herodotus. Henry was on his own, and whether he knew it or not, he was up against some professional page-turners, including Louis L'Amour and James Michener, each whispering in my ear to put that old misanthrope back on the shelf.

To my surprise, he held his own. Doubtless, the fact that I was several years older made a difference. Having—despite my unfortunate experience as a freshman—majored in American history, I knew a bit more about the world Henry inhabited, and I was able to decipher certain allusions that were lost on me the first time around. I can't say that I had sufficiently greater life experiences to allow me to fully appreciate the sense of failure that hung over one who, though an eminent historian, had never lived up to the standard of accomplishment established by his grandfather and great-grandfather, both presidents of the United States and distinguished diplomats. Nor had I reached an age when technology feels foreign and threatening, the property of generations younger than one's own— the feeling that provides the leitmotif for Adams's autobiography. But I had been out of college long enough to realize that one's education needn't—doesn't—stop upon leaving the classroom, and to gain at least an inkling of the broader sense in which Henry's title employed the term.

Most of all, however, I simply had the time to appreciate what Adams was doing in circling his subject the way he did, in speaking of himself as if he were someone else, in dropping names and places. To begin with, I took the time to read the introduction, which explained that the book was initially printed privately, intended for a select group of Adams's intimates who would understand his references and asides—and who might be offended if he lowered the veil of friendship too far. (This part of my own education, repeated in many other cases, led me to a bit of counterintuitive advice I now offer my students: If forced—by laziness or lack of time—to choose between reading the introduction to a required book, and reading the book itself, read the introduction. On first pass, you'll almost certainly get more out of it, and will save yourself a great deal of time. Of course, I simultaneously warn them that my tests will cover both.)

This intelligence alone—that Adams was writing for a select circle that didn't include me—might have been off putting, but instead it was liberating. If I didn't get Henry's jokes, it was because I wasn't supposed to get them. Consequently, every one I did decipher counted to my credit, rather than merely mitigating my blame. At the same time, the knowledge that Adams was writing for this small circle actually broadened the impact of his message, and the meaning of his education. Most memoirists employ the first-person in recounting their lives; and though this lends an immediacy to their tales, it also draws a clear distinction between them and everyone else. (Put otherwise, the distance between first and second person is greater than between second and third.) By substituting "he" for "I," Adams wrote as though his protagonist might have been anyone, or at least anyone in his circle. This wasn't a large group, to be sure, but, centered as it was on the homes of Adams and John Hay, across Lafayette Square from the White House, it played an important role in American national affairs—sometimes active, sometimes observational—during the second half of the nineteenth century. And the concerns Adams felt—for the Union during the Civil War, for public virtue during the Gilded Age, for faith during the Darwinian revolution, for decorum during the Populist decade—were concerns shared among an entire generation that felt itself heir to, and custodian of, the achievements of the Founders.

I can't say I entirely captured Henry Adams on the high plains of Wyoming; he was too subtle for that. But I did capture a good glimpse of him—enough of a glimpse that I kept coming back to his schoolroom every few years for the next twenty-five (and counting). Sometimes I paid professional visits: Whenever my writing dealt with the late nineteenth century, I checked what Henry had to say on my subject. Invariably he said something worth quoting. Of Ulysses Grant's scandalously disappointing presidency, Adams remarked, "The progress of evolution from President Washington to President Grant was alone evidence enough to upset Darwin." Regarding the psychic turmoil of the early 1890s, he extrapolated, persuasively, from his own circle to the country at large: "In 1892 neither [John] Hay, [Clarence] King, nor Adams knew whether they had attained success, or how to estimate it, or what to call it; and the American people seemed to have no clearer idea than they." When financial panic swept over the country the following year, producing the worst depression in American history to that point, he commented, "Even Henry Adams, who kept himself, as he thought, quite outside of every possible financial risk, had been caught in the cogs, and held for months over the gulf of bankruptcy, saved only by the chance that the whole class of millionaires were more or less bankrupt too, and the banks were forced to let the mice escape with the rats."

Yet my professional visits always led me to stay longer than I had anticipated, and, each time, I discovered more in Henry than I

knew before. His prose, so convoluted and confusing on first impression, came to seem like a garden path that drew one into its lushness;
though the path twisted as much as ever, my growing confidence that
Henry knew where he was going, even if I didn't, made the rambles
enjoyable rather than disconcerting.

Above all, the emotional depth of Henry's tale became more evident the more the balance of my own life shifted from future to
past. As my years ticked by, it was easier to understand the disappointments Henry felt on the passing of his own years—and not
simply the obvious disappointments of failure, but the less expected
and therefore more puzzling disappointments of success. By nearly
anyone's standard—including that of my freshman college professor
(and not entirely excluding those of Henry's famous ancestors,
whose presidencies were both terminated by popular rejection)—
Henry's life was a brilliant success. But still he felt out of place, adrift
in a world intended for others.

Henry has a couple of decades on me yet, and I have every reason to anticipate that our relationship will continue to evolve.
Meanwhile, what do I tell my own students? Naturally, that Henry
Adams is one of America's great writers, and that his autobiography
is a landmark of American letters. But I go on to say that I don't
expect them to understand, on first reading, more than a small part
of what Henry Adams is up to. And I secure, as best I can, a promise
from each of them not to get rid of the book at the end of the
semester but to save it for some moment years hence when Henry
won't be required and they will have the time to determine whether
his writing has improved with age.

BEN MARCUS

The Most Devastating Book I Read
THE EASTER PARADE by Richard Yates

Countries are devastated by floods and famine, buildings by
bombs, marriages by betrayal. These are real and tragic events
with long-term consequences that cannot be wished away. The
definition of devastation seems hardly debatable. My dictionary
says that to devastate is to destroy and render unrepairable.

Books cannot and maybe should not compete in this
realm. They might disturb us, but we can close them to stifle
their power. We can wish them away. They amount to a hallucination at best. It might come down to simple physics. We all
know what words and names can supposedly never do, how
harmless they are, inferior to sticks and stones, however much
a writer might dream otherwise. Books generally cannot shat-
ter a reader's life (writers are another matter). So if I speak of a

. . . .

Ben Marcus is the author of a novel, *Notable American Women*, and a
collection of stories, *The Age of Wire and String*. His work has
appeared in *Harper's, McSweeney's,* and *Fence,* and he teaches in the
graduate writing program at Columbia University.

devastating book, I must be exaggerating in order to emphasize something I feel and crave when I read—an exaggeration that is possibly grotesque, given the horror of real devastation. Why equate ourselves with actual and tragic ruin? Isn't it just twisted praise and corrupt language to brag of the damage a book wreaks, when no real damage ever occurs?

The fact is that some books have devastated me—destroyed and rendered unrepairable something inside me—and it is a feeling I would not trade for anything. It allows me to experience a crushing sadness that can seem to be the truest reaction to the central problem of being alive: mortality. Yet to walk the streets with this conscious knowledge is untenable and exhausting. A certain denial of our finite days is necessary in order to live with joy and energy and generosity. But this sadness I am advocating—from reading the most devastating writers—is exactly what enhances our joy, through its terrible contrast.

I am thinking in particular of the books of Richard Yates. He is a novelist who quietly and expertly breaks his readers' hearts so completely that the word "devastation" does not seem like hyperbole when used to describe his abilities. Perhaps this noun is imprecise, but it suggests that Yates can put us in mind of how temporary our lives are, how close to grief we constantly flirt. His characters are real people, desperately seeking happier days, wanting more for themselves than they will ever have. The devastation arises when we see his true and noble people do untrue and ignoble things, coming up short on a world they have promised themselves.

Books like *The Easter Parade* make us exist anew inside their world, where we flourish inside the skins of the characters. We experience the same colossal emotional devastation that they do, even though the whole enterprise is make-believe. We are wearing them and thus will drown when they do. It is this dreamed up version of myself getting trashed, a fantasy self that I am lulled into having who is then roughly, and brilliantly, taken away from me through the author's expertise. Good writers let us die inside their books so we might live more vividly in the outside world. We connect with a true reaction to the world that keeps us in mind of how deeply urgent it is to be alive, and the best books resonate long after we've read them. They stay in our past like wars we have fought to be better people.

It takes a special sort of writer to produce this emotional devastation. Anyone who would title one of his books *Eleven Kinds of Loneliness*, as Yates did, is going to sound like a connoisseur. It's an intriguing sort of authority to claim. What is it to specialize in loneliness? Does this mean he is good at it, the loneliest man alive? I'm afraid Richard Yates apparently was. He claimed *The Easter Parade* to be about his own life. But is loneliness something to succeed at? Or is Yates claiming a detached, anthropological perspective, loneliness as Dr. Spock might explain it?

The implication is that Yates has been there. But is there anyone who hasn't? I rather imagine that Yates did not suffer from detachment.

Guess what you want about me—I am a moping, cynical sad sack who will ruin every party with self-pitying words of gloom—but my criteria for books amounts to how plungingly sad they make me. I want that kind of early, big sadness that seemed to afflict not just me, but my entire neighborhood, an atmospheric virus bigger than my body. I actually miss that feeling, because it was one of the biggest feelings I ever had, a feeling I remember more for its size than anything else. The sadness becomes a physical symptom: my throat closes, my chest grows tight, sobs well up. The sky is a weight.

How odd, then, to admit that being sad is when I am happiest, when I can broadly indulge the feelings I am afraid to have in waking life. I want reading to feel like falling through the earth into the weeping pit, where I can cry my way through page after page until I emerge at the end of the book cleansed, raw, and filled with a new experience. Am I embarrassing you yet? This desire for an all-out Olympic literary sadness sometimes leads me to apologize, because there is another sort of reader, one who often appears in the same rooms as I do, whose hand I have to shake at parties, who argues that a book should uplift and delight and bring cheer. Shouldn't we want to feel better when we read, not worse? Who on Earth wants another reason to despair, a reminder of impending doom? The world is hard enough, let's not depress ourselves with sad books.

I used to say: Name a happy, positive, upbeat book that doesn't seem to be lying through its teeth about how life really is, and I'll shut up.

But that's too easy. Those supposedly happy books are just so, so sad.

Now I say this: Sadness is uplifting. Sadness is the new joy, devastation the new creation. Only false happiness is terribly sad. Who needs it? Sorrow is an affirmation, because it speaks to the serious problem of living for only a relatively short while in the world. We walk the streets knowing this is true, that we are mortal, but we have to forget that fact in order to live our lives. You're crazy if you're not occasionally sad. Let there be more truthful depictions of utter loneliness, for this is the most happiness-inducing kind. I feel worse when a writer lies to make things seem better than they are. I only feel better if the worst is not ignored.

It all sounds kind of backward, I guess, but what I'm arguing for is a kind of truth telling, however sad, in order for us to feel okay that we are in the hands of an author who also has fears. As a reader, I need to feel that it's being done, even if that truth might be complex or devastating. And it is this, ironically, that cheers me up.

In *The Easter Parade*, the sisters Emily and Sarah are what we might call good people. They want what we all often want: companionship, some happy times with reasonably kind people, a mother who is not crazy, a sense of belonging, independence.

Sarah, the cheerful and maybe simpler sister, takes the first romantic offer to come along, and marries into a long and terribly abusive relationship. She fades from the narrative as she slips from an active, cheerful life. The reader can then pity Sarah, but side with Emily, who seems smarter, more in the world, a college girl who has learned to want more for herself and to take her own needs seriously. She'll pull through, it seems certain, because this sort of person always does. We learned that example a long time ago; it's a myth that keeps us all striving to be better people. We can still believe that Sarah's decline is related to a set of bad choices she made.

This is where Yates kills us. You'll excuse my exaggeration. By creating two seemingly opposite characters in Sarah and Emily, we can initially think that their very different approaches to life will have equally different consequences. It's as simple as right and wrong. We get to choose which character to relate to, and for a while Yates makes that choice obvious, which only lulls us into complacency. Emily is bound to turn out for the better because she has taken control of her life, witnessed the erring ways of her overly devoted, alcoholic sister, and will now be what we all dream of being: strong, resilient, romantic but not dependent, a person with a series of intriguing jobs and intense relationships who travels and collects new experiences. We can then console ourselves that a certain moral path, if followed, could lead to happiness. It is comforting to know that a shared dream might be achieved.

What one sees in Yates is that even the good path, the earnest path, can lead to crushing despair, and sometimes this is undeniably, and painfully, true. This is part of what makes the world sad, however little we care to believe it. Really bad things can happen to good people. With Yates's characters, the better they are, the more decently they try to live, the more they see their hopes dashed and their chances dry up. The logic is vicious and not easy to stomach.

This is devastating in *The Easter Parade* because it prevents us from thinking we might ever be rewarded for our efforts in life. It warns us that no matter how well we live, no matter how much in love we are today, we could be eating cereal alone for dinner when we're sixty. There is just no way of knowing. And who, when you think about it, is not secretly afraid of this ending, an apartment-dwelling solitude with unemployment checks our only income? Yates makes you think for a while that no other outcome is even likely, but the upside is that we do things, we live, we have relationships, for their intrinsic pleasure, and not as a guarantee. His bleakness is in fact an argument for joy right now.

What gets devastated is the fiction that things will all work out, that everything's for the best, that we are being cared for. A deceit is being devastated, and we need books to perform this operation for us. As awful as this might sound as a literary experience, reading *The Easter Parade* might allow us to breathe and eat and live anew, to shake off complacency and appreciate the world around us, since Yates has demonstrated how potentially precarious our happiness truly is.

Emily's sad end comes despite her efforts. Through very little fault of her own, Emily has ended up poor and alone. Yates wrecks the myth that pulling yourself up by your bootstraps will set your life back on course and bring you some happiness. We see Emily pulling away throughout the novel, striving as diligently as she might to fulfill this dream, only to narrowly miss happiness. As her desperation increases, her chances diminish—a calculus of sadness that Yates can't keep himself from revealing. The novel ends with Emily verbally attacking her one remaining relative, a nephew who hardly knows her and who is her last resort. The scene is terrible, but utterly true, more so because it is ourselves we see, flailing and shouting on some quiet suburban street, with no money to our name, looking into the uncomprehending eyes of a distant relative whom we despise and love at once, because he is the closest thing we have to family, to home, to life.

Emily's last stand is a brave display of an exhausted person on the verge of some final and intolerable solitude. Her devastation is complete. At most, a reader will tour the ruins of this woman, sampling her unrepairable destruction, but this will be no judgmental detachment. Yates assures that we will never feel superior to such a person, since her path has been as strong, or stronger, than anything we might have mustered for ourselves.

LYDIA MILLET

The Most Apocalyptic Book I Read
THE WAR WITH THE NEWTS by Karel Čapek

The Apocalypse, Armageddon, the Rapture, the Day of Reckoning, the Last Judgment, the End Times: These are religious terms for the last desperate gasp of earthbound humankind, the moment at which man disappears from Earth and heaven is unveiled, the end of history and the beginning of eternity. It's a staggering pageant: plagues, pestilence, famine; the oceans and rivers run red with blood, fiery dragons rear their monstrous seven heads above the horizon, the four horsemen soar down from aloft blowing trumpets.

The seductive power of religious myths of the Apocalypse turns on the notion that the epic moment, the final gathering of souls, brings enlightenment. (The word "apocalypse," in fact, comes from the Greek *apokalypsis*, meaning "uncovering"

. . . .

Lydia Millet is the author of three novels, most recently *My Happy Life*. Millet lives in the desert outside Tucson, Arizona, where she writes on environmental issues for organizations such as the Center for Biological Diversity.

or "revelation.") At the end of time, evil is traded in for good. The face of God is revealed. A vast and endless comprehension is gained, followed by the happily-forever-after for which we believe ourselves always to have dreamed. Finally, after the long struggle of history, the squalor, the fear, the tormenting inescapable conflicts of social life and the self, the question of whether in fact meaning exists at all, all questions are answered, and the answer is simple. Come in, my child, and be at peace. For this reason, understandably, the apocalyptic faithful welcome the End Times.

For very different reasons, I've been hung up on the end of time for what seems like forever. When I was twelve, I cried at the sight of nuclear explosions playing on old newsreels, which they showed us, for some reason, in biology class instead of physics. I remember how a small group of self-righteous girls, some of whom were my friends, refused to watch the footage on the grounds that it was "traumatic" and they should not be exposed to it. I remember the terrible beauty of the mushroom cloud blossoming and spreading as it towered over the landscape beneath. As infinite in their variety as snowflakes, all mushroom clouds are nonetheless only one.

I was living in Toronto then and by thirteen was marching against U.S. missile testing in Canada. Now, at thirty-three, I'm still grappling with the sublime, apocalyptic image of the mushroom cloud. My fascination has become my life, for the past couple of years and probably several more to come. I'm writing a book about the men who built the first atom bomb, and I'm about to fly to Hiroshima and Nagasaki to see the monuments to the bomb victims and talk to survivors. The apocalypse weighs heavy. Yet the secular apocalypses that haunt my generation are different from the religious visions of the past. They, too, offer grand spectacles: nuclear holocaust, global warming, ozone depletion, the wholesale collapse of environmental life-support systems, hurtling asteroids and comets, viral epidemics—take your pick. But postmodern projections of the end of time carry few promises of holy vision, redemption or understanding.

Hollywood takes these more "realistic" disaster scenarios and runs with them—and, typically, Hollywood narratives of the secular apocalypse retain vestiges of the biblical Apocalypse's enlightenment paradigm. Action figures like Bruce Willis can save the world only from, say, a fiery asteroid once they make peace with errant family members and accept their own mortality. Sacrificing their individual lives to prevent global death, the apocalyptic heroes—whose personal emotional lives are apparently of such gigantic and paramount importance that they can redeem all of humanity—lend meaning to what would otherwise be a bleak cinematic vision, devoid of meaning and of even the pretense of moral authority.

Despite my fascination with secular apocalypses—the bad kind, you might say—I've hardly ever found a worthwhile apocalyptic story that doesn't devolve into a hackneyed lesson about the need to find love and improve yourself. With one exception.

I first encountered the bulgy-eyed protagonists of Karel Čapek's 1937 novel *The War with the Newts* when I was in my early twenties, living in LA and working for slave wages as a copyeditor for Larry Flynt. *Andrias Scheuchzeri,* a species of newt first discovered (according to the book) by a ship captain in the waters off a remote island near Sumatra, was a salamander capable of walking upright—as well as synthesizing information and acquiring human language. His creator, Czech writer Karel Čapek, is best known as the man who made up the word "robot." A brilliant humorist and allegorist, Čapek was also a journalist in post–World War I Prague, a contemporary of the more inwardly turned Franz Kafka, and one of the most imaginative early writers of science fiction. He was a pragmatic and actively political writer. "Literature that does not care about reality or about what is really happening to the world," he wrote, "literature that is reluctant to react as strongly as word and thought allow, is not for me." *The War with the Newts* was his last novel; the best English translation is by M. and R. Weatherall.

Čapek's newts are naive, childlike specimens when first encountered in the wild and put to work diving for pearls by the greedy, paternalistic Captain van Toch. Standing about the height of a "ten-year-old boy," the newts have hands, tails, and a habit of smacking their lips; when they first meet humans they stand up on their hind legs in shallow water, wriggle, and emit a clicking, hissing bark that sounds like *ts, ts*. Pitifully eager to please, they're subjugated, tortured, and often massacred with impunity; their trusting natures make them the perfect victims.

Packed into filthy cargo ships to die of starvation or infection, bred for servitude, sent to zoos and work farms and animal research labs, the newts gradually learn to distrust. But before they rebel, many are assimilated into human culture. With innocent admiration for the accomplishments of their human captors, they adopt bourgeois customs; study etiquette; and enroll in universities, sometimes becoming respected scholars who—because they live mostly in water—have to deliver their lectures from bathtubs. Young female newts, who attend a finishing school wearing makeshift skirts donated by decency-loving matrons, come to worship their headmistress as a saint. And one tourist couple vacationing in the Galápagos encounters an earnest newt who goes nowhere without his well-thumbed copy of *Czech for Newts*, a phrasebook he has memorized. "This booklet . . . has become my dearest companion," the newt tells the Czech couple, and proceeds to grill them on the details of Czech history. "I should like to stand myself on the sacred spot where the Czech noblemen were executed, as well as on the other famous places of cruel injustice." When the pearls the newts have customarily harvested for their masters become scarce, the newts themselves become the world's most important commodity, traded by the tens of millions on the stock exchange.

Different categories of newts fetch different prices: there are Leading, Heavy, Team, Odd Jobs, Trash, and Spawn newts, with the Leading being intelligent, trained leaders of labor columns and the Trash being "inferior, weak, or physically defective newts." Newt farms all along the coastlines of the world produce newts by the millions—until finally the newts' undersea civilization expands and industrializes so extensively that newts far outnumber and outgun humans. Unfortunately for the human race, newts require coastlines: Only there, in the shallow water, can they live. As their population explodes, they run out of coast.

And so the "earthquakes" begin. Cataclysmic seismic activity across Gulf states from Texas to Alabama is referred to as "the Earthquake in Louisiana" and soon followed by earthquakes in China and Africa. Finally European radio stations pick up a croaking voice, and Chief Salamander begins to speak: "Your explosives have done well. We thank you. Hello, you people!" He explains that the newts have run out of room and will be forced to break down the continents to create more living space. Indifferent to human welfare, the newt civilization is driven by a mindless urge to expand. "The mountains will be pulled down last," says Chief Salamander. "Hello, you men. Now we shall send out light music from your gramophones."

Characteristically, the humans interpret this warning as a "stupid and vulgar joke" and do not listen; and so begins the salamandrine apocalypse.

The genius of *The War with the Newts* lies less in its plot or its wry political wisdom than in its exceptional newt portraiture. The talking salamanders are at least half-human, since *Andrias Scheuchzeri* walks and talks more or less like *Homo sapiens*. Their anthropomorphic charm makes them unforgettable: As exaggerations of pragmatic, economic modern man, they're as devoid of passion as they are devoid of morality. The newts are a kind of soulless and adorable child, horrifyingly mechanical but at the same time guileless. And then there's the sense of humor of their creator, which imbues them with the power to convey to us, without preaching or tear jerking, the plausibility—even the overwhelming mundanity—of apocalyptic endings.

Because, of course, it's only partly the newts that bring about the end of human civilization. Citing economic necessity, the nations of the world refuse to stop arming them or supplying them with tools or explosives. The human race cannot see past the end of its nose, and as a result shoots itself in the foot; obviously the newts' drive to grow and expand only mirrors that of their human tutors.

Čapek makes clear that the apocalypse, when and if it comes, is bound to be a man-made event, as much a product of human ingenuity as Velcro, cotton candy, or the iBook I'm using to write this. He makes the chilling proposal that religious apocalypses have it right in envisioning a human end that is the result of a profound moral, ethical, and spiritual failure. Where they may be wrong, his book suggests, is in envisioning a light at the end of the apocalyptic tunnel. In a time when total war, among other evils, has become commonplace, it seems desperately wishful and absurdly convenient to think that all our mistakes and crimes will deliver us neatly into the hands of an infinite benevolence.

And that's the brilliance of *The War with the Newts*: it shows us how romantic, how wistful, how hopeful, and even optimistic the old-fashioned religious Apocalypse begins to look when we compare it to the apocalypses we've come to know lately. In our world, expediency is the engine that propels destruction; mass murder is done in the name of, say, cheap oil for our cars, and no American appears to doubt the rationality of this. Since time immemorial, we tell our-selves, man has fought over goods, man has wanted as much for himself as he could grab, man has found it more efficient to plunder others than transform himself. It's business as usual.

So it is in the world of *The War with the Newts*. If a species needs more room, it takes it; any "collateral damage" is unfortunate. Čapek's newts are a product of European literary culture, but in one respect they look a lot like Americans. Driven by the cold and calcu-lating expansionist capitalism that seems to guide the hand of our government far and above any concept of God—no matter how often the name of God is bandied about, on dollar bills or in tele-vised speeches—these are beings that act in a single dimension. Because the shibboleth of "economic growth" has taken the place of God as a good unto itself, a pure imperative, it overrides all else— matters of art and aesthetics, matters of social welfare and the integrity of communities, matters of the spirit and human commun-ion with whatever forces or ideas are held to be divine.

The last chapter of *The War with the Newts* consists of a discus-sion Čapek holds with himself. How can he leave the reader with such a bleak vision of the future? Isn't there hope? Shouldn't a book have an ending that offers, if not salvation, at least the suggestion that meaning is inherent to human destiny?

These are questions most writers face—one reason Čapek's dia-logue resonates. I've occasionally been accused of writing in too "grim" or even "depraved" an idiom, the latter of which I have to admit caused delight. I've been accused of writing about "unlikable characters" or succumbing to "negativity," and books of mine have gone unpublished because they allegedly suffer from the curse of "darkness." To the question of whether he should write a book with a happy ending, Čapek says sorry, but he's just being honest. The apocalypse isn't his fault; he warned us. The world will end, but "at least it will be accomplished with the help of the science, industry, and public opinion, with the application of all human ingenuity! No cosmic catastrophe, nothing but state, official, economic, and other causes. Nothing can be done to prevent it."

In other words, the modern apocalypse, robbed of revelation, just isn't a happy ending. And happy endings are what we crave. The recipe for contemporary stories demands a generous dollop of redemption; readers require not only the promise of meaning but also the promise of being saved. Our love of apocalyptic stories makes clear that we're a deeply religious culture robbed of ready outlets for the expression of spiritual longing. Governed by secular overlords, we're desperate to find ourselves touched and saved—if not in our daily lives, then at the very least in myths and fables. In everything we consume we seem to look for a glimpse of transfiguration, for reassurance that we are part of a common whole. But when it comes to politics, to economics, to the ethics of the so-called real world, we throw up our hands and claim we're not part of the whole. It is too vast, too multiple to include us. We're tiny people who can do nothing, and therefore have nothing to do.

It is in this way, with the proverbial whimper, that history threatens to grind to a halt, leaving in its wake only a shimmering silence.

NASDIJ

The Saddest Book I Read

TO TAME A LAND by Louis L'Amour

I was living on a remote cow ranch in the Gila Wilderness area of New Mexico. I was finally on my own, and independent, although I was still an adolescent. Green around the gills (which means girls still intimidated me). My job was mainly in the barn. The cowboys were smart to put me in the barn. I did not fail there. I took care of the horses, and I lived in the bunkhouse with the other cowboys. Real cowboys. The kind that came with dirt and thistle burrs. Not the Hollywood kind who took their baths with Miss Kitty's whores upstairs in the saloon. No. We took our baths in an old tin tub with the other cowboys. We did not have television. The picture show was far away. We played checkers on the porch of the bunkhouse, but mainly we read books. We passed them around among the cowboys.

· ·

Nasdijj was raised on reservations and in migrant camps all across America. He is totally self-taught and works as a volunteer with children living with AIDS. He has published two memoirs: *The Blood Runs Like a River Through My Dreams* and *The Boy and the Dog are Sleeping*.

The cowboys wrote poetry, too. Long tales of hurt and sadness, mainly. Go figure. Loneliness eats at you. Then, you accept it. I did. We drove our trucks up to Nevada where there was a poetry festival. We walked out on the stage and read our work. This was not a tobacco-chewing illiterate group of mindless grunts. This was a tobacco-chewing literate group of mainly silent grunts. Grunts who wrote things, and they could read. There was a lot of time for me to read books out in that barn.

We did not check our books out from the library (no one had a card) because that would mean returning them every two weeks, and leaving the ranch every two weeks was impossible. On long cow drives, you could be hundreds of miles from the nearest library, let alone a road. So, we bought our books from a book club. They arrived in the mail.

The cowboys had favorites. Ernest Hemingway (he could hold you) was at the top of the list. Everything by Hemingway had been passed around until the books were worn thin as boards. Louis L'Amour was down one notch from Hemingway. The cowboys liked to read L'Amour just to see if he got it right, and he did not.

To Tame a Land made its slow way to me out in the barn. It was handed to me with a warning. The cowboy who had just finished it called it sad. "I don't think L'Amour likes Indians much," he said.

I knew what this meant. It meant indifference. Indians were window dressing. If that.

That ranch in the Gila was not a place (I cannot speak for other ranches) where overt racism was exactly alive and well. No one had an inclination for such social nonsense. You learned to work— hard—with all sorts of different folks. The literature of the West often paints the place with some oblique, toughened whiteness, but I never knew where that place was. I figured most writers who wrote about the West were not from the West. An overt racist on our ranch would have been in the wrong cowboy business. We had black cowboys, Hispanic cowboys (who claimed a rather severe Spanish heritage), Apache cowboys, Mexican cowboys (who were not legal), and I was partly Navajo—no one asked although I rarely thought about it. No one cared. No one could tell the white cowboys from the other cowboys, as the cow dirt that covered everything equalized all notions of color and race.

In fact, we had to share the limited supply of hot water (which was heated in a pot on the wood stove) in the old tin tub. That tin tub was a permanent fixture on the front porch where the cowboys soaked the cowpoke dirt off their bodies, played checkers, and read their books.

Our small collection of books, on a bookshelf in the bunkhouse, was regarded like a sacred shrine. You took real good care of the books themselves or you paid for it with the wrath of cowboys, which meant you took your bath last. By then, the water would be as thick as mud, and it was cold, too.

You could either do your job, or you could not. No one cared spit if you had been to school. You either worked hard or you were asked to leave. Men who could not or would not work hard were dangerous. They had accidents, and other people got hurt. Intolerance and things like hangovers were not tolerated any more than bad books were regarded with delight.

The books of Louis L'Amour, such as the one that had been handed to me with a warning ("sadder than a dead dog" is what the cowboy actually said), typically sold ten million to twelve million copies per book, and L'Amour had written dozens of them. Our opinion of L'Amour began to change. "It was Indian country," L'Amour writes in *To Tame a Land*, "and when our wagon wheel busted none of them would stop to help us."

Fancy that.

"There was mighty little to see. It was a long rolling grass plain wherever a body looked."

This implied emptiness. As cowboys we knew this: Emptiness was what usually came from inside a man; it was not usually an external phenomenon.

By page four, our twelve-year-old hero, whose name is Rye, is killing Indians. "My shooting had caught them flat-footed. I'd killed me two Indians, and all in less than a minute."

I was seventeen and looked upon the shenanigans of a twelve-year-old with suspicion. I chewed on this publishing silliness something considerable in the old tin tub. I had seen a few Indians in my time, and none of them were flat-footed. Quite the opposite.

So. This is what they meant when white people talked about the Great Mythology of the West. I thought it racial rhetoric. But ten to twelve million other folks did not share my minority opinion. Louis L'Amour was one of the most prolific yarn spinners of his time and definitely put his literary stamp on the romance of the cowboy.

Where I lived, the Indians were the cowboys.

By page five, our protagonist's parents have been murdered in cold blood (by you-know-who), and Rye has killed more than a few Indians himself on his dusty road of fate to become a gunslinger (Doc Holliday and all the other usuals make appearances), but . . . "The night smelled good. There were a million stars in the sky, looked like, and I could feel the soft wind over the grass."

No time to mourn. Gunslingers do not grieve. They just get on with it. This image of the male is bunk.

I saw cowboys cry their eyes out when they lost puppies or foals.

So much for the literate reflections of a twelve-year-old hero. I personally did not know a single twelve-year-old I would trust with a gun, let alone a slew of firearms. We did not wear guns. I cannot think of a single time we shot anything. And hit it.

Beer cans would not run for their lives.

L'Amour has all the cowboys crack shots like a swat team. Dead, dumb Indians everywhere. His book is a sea of death. The literature of genocide. The cowboy who handed me the book was right. It was sad.

I decided I would become a writer. If L'Amour could do it, I could do it. Better. I would tell my version of the truth. In *To Tame a Land*, our hero, Rye, grows to be thirteen. By chapter 4, he's on to killing white men (just the bad ones), and he's counting them in notches. No notches for the Indians. They merit not a passing thought.

I would not even mention this piece of sad fiction except for the fact that the accumulated weight of fictions just like it, when added up, form a picture of a place that never was, and a time that never happened. Most Indians did not die in battle with heroic white folks. Nor were they killed by gunslingers. They were killed by diseases that ravaged entire cultures.

The history of the West is the history of disease. Ask any cowboy who fears the coming of foot-and-mouth disease. The sad reality is that Indians are still dying from diseases. The disease of violence (drug gangs have arrived at many reservations) is prime, now, as a major cause of death among young Indian men, and chances are that if someone else does not kill you, you will kill yourself. Suicide is a major problem, but L'Amour never wrote about that.

Fictions like this are murderous. They pass off illusion as fact, stereotype as portraiture. L'Amour's counterfeit comes to be seen as the genuine article. It kills people. It kills culture. It kills even the shadow of truth.

In *To Tame a Land*, our hero, Rye, becomes a mountain man, herds cattle, goes to town, meets a woman, hunts buffalo. This is odd. By this time—the time of the big cattle drives through such places as Texas and New Mexico—the buffalo were gone, and the mountain men (such as Kit Carson, who makes an appearance here) were a memory. By the time the cowboys came along who rode the big cattle drives that became the economic, driving engine of the West, the only thing "wild" out here were the coyotes. Most of the folks who owned the land (county court records always bear this out) were speculators who lived in London.

Our gunslinger hero, now fifteen, lives for a time in an Apache wickiup, a tribal hut made from mud and sticks, and a particularly ironic contrivance as by this time in history, the Chiricahua had been shipped away to prisons for the crime of allegedly leaving the reservation, and there were very few people living in wickiups, let alone wickiups in or anywhere near Tucson, which is where all of this romantic nonsense supposedly takes place. Tucson would have been the last place a fifteen-year-old white boy would have found himself living the life of an Apache in a wickiup. Not even as rebellion. At the end of a cattle drive, our gunslinger (now sixteen and having left the wickiup) makes ten thousand bucks.

That was rich—a real side slapper. We did not make ten thousand bucks on a cattle drive, and it caused us to look up the cost of beef in the late 1800s. From what we could figure, Rye might have made fifty bucks. In the late 1800s, fifty bucks was a lot of money. For a cowboy, it still is.

By seventeen, Rye's a whiskey drinker. It's good for him. Puts hair on his chest. YOU drink that much whiskey and try getting up at four in the morning to tend to cows and horses. Notwithstanding the ravages of puberty, it cannot be done.

I started reading sections of this fantastic book aloud in the tin tub to the other cowboys so we could all laugh. But behind the laughter there was a sadness, too. This was supposedly our history, and the thing was cow manure. We liked where we lived, what we did for a living. There was a matter of choice and responsibility in it that never gets communicated in the books about the West where fate is a sore, long trail of eating dust, and events just happen (like attacks from Indians), and you cope as fate unfolds. This was not the life we knew, and we were the cowboys. We did not know what Rye was. But we felt sorry for him.

The book cowboys never wash dishes. We did a lot of that.

In the end, Rye gets the girl.

That was it for us. Tobacco spit.

"And that was the way it was," L'Amour tells us, "in the old days before the country grew up and men put their guns away. There may come a time when the western hills are empty again, and the land will go back to the wilderness, and the hard old ways. The guns are hung up. The cows roam fat and lazy. But the spirit is still there, just as it was when the longhorns came up from Texas, and the boys washed the creeks for gold."

Gold. All we had was an old tin tub. And the western hills, we knew, were never really empty. People lived there, even if you rarely saw them. Animals lived there, too. Emptiness was a convenient illusion. We put our books away (especially L'Amour), and took out our journals, and our poetry, and our loose-leaf notebooks, our pens and our pencils, and proceeded to tell (in silence, which was our way) the stories of our lives, and when spring came, we would drive our trucks up briefly to Nevada in our cowboy boots, where we would march our courage to the sticking place, a stage, and we would tell our sadness to the world.

BRET LOTT

The Most Fragile Book I Read
THE CATCHER IN THE RYE by J. D. Salinger

I wanted to be a forest ranger. But the forestry program I enrolled in my freshman year at Northern Arizona University had less to do with nature than with producing future executives for Weyerhaeuser and Georgia-Pacific.

I went back home and enrolled at Cal State Long Beach. I became a marine biology major. Then I got a D in a physics course I needed at least a C in.

I quit college, became an RC Cola salesman for no good reason other than that was what my father had been. I figured it was a way to make money. Maybe it was the career I'd been headed for all along. I knew RC Cola inside and out.

But after a year of selling soda pop, I felt like a phony. Every time I walked in a grocery store to talk some phony into buying a phony product no one really needed, I found myself

. . . .

Bret Lott has published nine books, including the novels *A Song I Knew by Heart*, *The Hunt Club,* and *Jewel* (an Oprah's Book Club Selection). He is writer in residence at the College of Charleston in South Carolina.

longing for college and a life that perhaps might have meaning beyond the claustrophobic world of all these phonies around me.

I had Tuesday nights free, and the only class with an opening at my local community college was creative writing. I signed up for it.

The teacher was a wild-haired, Harley-riding poet/professor from Cal State. I sat at my desk, just off work and in my RC uniform, the wide blue tie with the swirly red-and-white logo at the very tip, the navy blue polyester workpants, the black leather steel-toed shoes.

Everyone else in the class was in civilian attire, and more than once the poet/prof looked at me in my uniform, and smirked.

Then one night he assigned a novel whose very title made everyone around me beam. I'd never heard of it. I went home, this novel with the oddball title—*The Catcher in the Rye*—in hand. I lay on the old, beat-up sofa in the front room of the house I shared with three friends, two of them surfers, the other a seminary student, and started reading this story about a kid named Holden Caulfield.

He was a good-hearted and well-meaning, if a bit prickly, sixteen-year-old who had been kicked out of prep school. It's the late 1940s, New York City, and he's supposed to be heading home to his parents' apartment. But he decides instead to sort of run away and try to live some kind of life that might make sense for as long as he can in a world infested with phonies. I kept reading there on the sofa—and kept reading and reading and reading on through the night, reading this amazing book, this totally true book, this genuinely real book, told by Holden with an urgency and intimacy I'd never encountered before.

This was me, this Holden Caulfield. This was me, "surrounded by jerks," me and Holden both oppressed by and shackled to a life that didn't allow us any power of our own. This was me, too, "the most terrific liar you ever saw in your life," as Holden informed me he was at the start of things—I was a soda pop salesman (who in his right mind needs soda pop?); and here was me, too, dreaming about just the right girl and knowing it wasn't going to happen.

All of this was me, despite the fact Holden was there in postwar New York City and getting drinks and a hotel room and a hooker (sort of), then ice skating innocently enough with Sally Hayes, who was wearing "this little blue butt-twitcher of a dress."

He was right about everything, this Holden Caulfield, even if he was a little bit brittle, psychologically speaking: The world really is full of jerks and phonies, and innocence was being stripped from us every time we turned around, and the only thing it seemed we could possibly do was to try and save someone we loved (for Holden, it was his younger sister Phoebe), to "catch a body comin' through the rye."

This was about me, the me that had been drifting for what felt like so many years, from one hope for a future to another to another—park ranger to biologist to salesman to uniformed geek in a classroom of wannabe writers, chief among them this poet/prof and his smirk.

I sat up, there in the house I lived in, and suddenly I was in a different room, in a different house, on a different beat-up sofa. The world was different now.

All because of this book, this true book. This book was solid. "Right on, Holden!" I wanted to shout to the house, to my job, to that creative writing class, even if my housemates were asleep, the phonies. Tell it like it is, Holden!

Then, I grew older.

Eventually, I became a writer myself.

I reread *The Catcher in the Rye* four or five more times during the next several years, holding it dearer each time, admiring it more the deeper I went into my own life as a writer. It's no easy feat, let me tell you, to pull off a first-person voice as sharp and moving and quick and believable as Holden's, nor is it a simple endeavor to infuse the few days over which the story takes place with as much life and confusion and as many full-blooded characters as Salinger does.

But more important than Salinger's art was Holden's idealism: Each time I reread the book I wanted nothing more than to again be Holden, still raging against the way the world wanted to swallow all of us whole.

My family had begun to grow, we moved here and there at the whim of teaching jobs, and we were continually stone broke. Next-door neighbors held parties that ended up as brawls outside our back door; student papers nagged to be graded every waking moment, the five classes of remedial English I taught sometimes feeling more a baby-sitting job for the semiliterate than actual teaching; rejections of my stories piled up like leaves off a tree.

And we had two children—two boys—whose presence in our lives amplified the whole notion of meaning: Here were two new human beings on planet Earth, two new people whose paths through the world jungle we all inhabit had to be blazed by my wife and myself, while we ourselves were trying to blaze paths of our own.

For a few dark years, we had to put them in day care full-time, from eight in the morning until six at night, just so that we could make ends meet. Those boys grew, and there came a day for each when he no longer wanted to hold my hand when we walked across the street, or from the car to the grocery store or from here to anywhere.

Later still, my writing life took a strange twist when Oprah Winfrey selected my novel *Jewel* for her book club. I found myself one evening not long ago sitting in a leather chair in a room we call the library in a new house we'd bought, and holding in my lap a first edition of *The Catcher in the Rye*.

It had been maybe fifteen years since I'd last reread the book. I wanted to revisit the old urgency, the old idealism, the old sense of true, of solid, of "Right on Holden!" I'd had visited upon me the night this all began.

I wanted to see the old me. The one before leather chairs and first editions. The me that raged against all the phonies out there.

I read—and read and read and read. And here was the same old urgency, the same brash assessment of everyone and everything as phony, the same longing for love and the same desire to save the innocent.

But it was a different book this time—a better book, an even truer book, for a certain passage early on, a passage I had of course read before, but which only now revealed the length and width and depth of this young kid's, this child's, perplexity at the fragility of life.

Here is that passage, in which Holden allows himself and us the briefest of glimpses into the inner reaches of his heart:

I was only thirteen, and they were going to have me psychoanalyzed and all, because I broke all the windows in the garage the night he died, and I broke all the goddamn windows with my fist, just for the hell of it. I even tried to break all the windows in the station wagon we had that summer, but my hand was already broken and everything by that time, and I couldn't do it. It was a very stupid thing to do, I'll admit, but I hardly didn't even know I was doing it, and you didn't know Allie.

Allie. His brother, younger by two years, who died of leukemia when Holden was thirteen.

I sat up, there in the house I lived in, and suddenly I was in a different room, in a different house, on a different leather chair. The world was different now.

This story, I saw there in the comfy confines of the library and leather chair and adulthood, was about a child's grief, plain and simple, and in that moment, too, the book suddenly became infinitely larger. Sure, I'd known he was brittle before this; sure, I'd known his little brother had died each time I'd read the book before this. But those early readings had been filled with me, at the center of my life.

This was a book written for me, yet again. Me, a parent of two children on the very edge of being grown-up themselves. How would I feel if one of my sons had died, and the other—in the throes of his grief, in the face of the irreconcilable and inconsolable truth that the phonies live and the innocent die—what if my son broke every window in the garage, beat on the windows of the van until his hand was broken and bleeding?

And I loved Holden even more. But now not only for his fierce rage against the phonies of the world, but also and even more dearly for the fragile state from which that rage emanates: Holden knows firsthand the black and nonreturnable gift of grief.

When will my own sons know this gift? I was forced to wonder.

The world was different, yet again.

This is the most fragile book I have ever read. Fragile because in the initial rush of its ferocious beauty, the young who read it—myself included—can see Holden as their spokesman against the machine, yet in the same instant Holden is himself utterly breakable, because beneath that fearless veneer bent on exposing the world in all its pretension, is a fearful child. Inside that ferocious stance is a broken heart.

Now, although I still want to shout "Right on Holden!" despite the embarrassingly archaic sound of the rallying cry of my youth, I also want to whisper, "Be careful, Holden." I want to say, "Please hold my hand."

My older son is leaving for college, his freshman year, in two weeks. "Be careful, Zeb," I have resolved to say, but also, "Tell it like it is!"

And, because of this book, because of the strength of its truth—we will all lose our innocence, and grief will come upon us—I will also say, "Please hold my hand."

JILL McCORKLE

The Most Beautiful Book I Read
SHOT IN THE HEART by Mikal Gilmore

It might sound odd to describe *Shot in the Heart* as the most beautiful book I read. After all, it is Mikal Gilmore's unflinching story of his brother Gary, a career criminal and cold-blooded murderer who fell before a Utah firing squad in 1977. It's a horrifying, and riveting tale. But beautiful?

My dictionary defines the adjective as "having qualities which delight the senses" and "exciting intellectual or emotional admiration." Keats described it eloquently enough in 1819: "Beauty is truth, truth beauty,—that is all/ ye know on earth, and all ye need to know"—although it certainly wasn't the first time the concept was voiced.

And it seems at the very heart of this concept is the word "truth." Combine definitions and you easily come to emotional truth—that shining moment every writer is hoping to find. The

....

Jill McCorkle teaches in the master's program at Bennington College in Vermont. Her eighth book is the short story collection *Creatures of Habit*.

word "beautiful," in its truest form, means that it appeals to the senses at large, perhaps in a way that surpasses what we are so easily able to see, hear, taste, feel.

That is what *Shot in the Heart* represents for me. It is beautiful in terms of construction, the lyrical language and masterful weaving of past and present, but it also achieves a level of beauty thematically as the author takes his tragic family legacy and finds within it a truth that, in turn, lends a kind of acceptance—and, therefore, a kind of grace and strength—that has enabled him to move forward with his own life.

But it is also beautiful to me because through his story, Mikal Gilmore answered questions that troubled, haunted, and intrigued me all of my life. It has as much to do with my reading of the book as with Gilmore's writing.

I grew up in a nice town in a family that loved me. But Lumberton, North Carolina, was a close neighbor to Fayetteville, where a distinguished army doctor named Jeffrey MacDonald snapped one night and murdered his family. His crime haunted people for a long, long time, and I daresay it still does. I find myself referring to it in my fiction; I find that in looking back on some of the sweetest summer nights of my childhood, this tragedy lurks at the edges, a reminder of the fragility of our safety.

As a child, I was particularly aware of the crimes committed regularly in our county. I didn't want to hear all about it, but I did want to. I had to hide my eyes during episodes of *The Twilight Zone* but I wouldn't have missed it for anything. I was an obsessive witness. I was that way about The Boston Strangler and Charles Manson. After I heard that Manson had been crouched and hiding in a tiny kitchen cabinet when apprehended, I routinely checked the whole kitchen before going to bed. I checked under the bed. Behind the shower curtain. I checked into the darkest recesses my own mind could conjure. I once scared myself so bad while taking a shower in my college dorm that I took off running and fell flat on my face and skinned the entire surface of my body. I don't even remember what it was I was thinking about, only that I had successfully taken my emotional state off the chart. I was married for five years when my husband asked what I was ever going to do if I actually found someone under the bed during my nightly check. It did not even occur to me that I sank to my knees and looked every night—finding enough dust bunnies to frighten a good housekeeper for sure, but no men intent on murder and mayhem.

So why do I race to read every criminal profile I can find? I didn't understand it myself until I saw Stephen King being interviewed on television. As a kid, he said, he became obsessed with a gruesome crime and the psychopath who had committed it. It wasn't for any kind of thrill for violence; rather, it was out of fear and the desire to understand what makes such a person tick. He thought: If I can recognize such a person, I'll be safe. If I can name it, it can't hurt me. I found myself sitting up straight and nodding with his every word. That was exactly how I had always felt.

I imagine that the desire for such understanding is what led Mikal Gilmore to tell his story. By somehow defining and giving a permanent sense of truth to his brother's life, he would be able to leave its tragedy behind him.

Shot in the Heart is the story of family history and legends and myths: the bloody sacrifices and superstitions of an old Mormon heritage, the supernatural tales of ghosts and untimely deaths attributed to a family curse, domestic violence, and abuse. And yet, Mikal Gilmore, who was quite a bit younger than his three brothers, escaped the harshest circumstances. The same father who had regularly beaten the mother and been abusive to his sons in earlier years was, for the author, an old man who, for whatever reason, took an interest in him. Mikal was aware of Gary's jealousy for what was a much easier life, and he in turn felt a kind of survivor's guilt. Yet he also felt a regret for not being a part of their family, no matter how horrible the costs.

Emotionally, this book recognizes and acknowledges everything that any writer needs to know and understand. That no two individuals share the exact same existence. That a feeling of relief or hope or happiness relies heavily on the knowledge of what lies on the other side. The more accurate the portrayal of what is dark, the more enlightened the reader is about what is good. The truest human emotions cannot be isolated and simplified without examining all that feeds into the end result, which automatically means that the picture is anything but simple.

We read newspaper accounts about strangers who commit horrific crimes. We are shocked. Sometimes the shock subsides and a routine day takes over. But sometimes we think, "What if?" or, "That could have been me." Then it is not so easy to see the world the same way again.

It is in this very way that Mikal Gilmore tells his brother's story. With just a few slight changes, it could have been his own story. As a teacher of creative writing, these are the very ideas and questions I want students to explore. It is easy to produce a portrait of pure evil or goodness, yet neither represents reality. When you have a character who is perfect, you must go in and find the dark spot. Where is this person morally weak? What injustice has he or she produced? Was there a time when he should have spoken and didn't, or spoke when he shouldn't have? The answers are there, and anything marring the surface will only make the rest of the picture credible. In the same way, an evil character has to have a weak spot—some vulnerable moment when he genuinely loved someone or was lonely or ridiculed.

Sometimes it is difficult to find the moment that can evoke human compassion, but it is most definitely there. I have often used the likes of Charles Manson or Jeffrey Dahmer—monsters of our society—as examples. And maybe you have to push all the way back to when the man was an infant—completely innocent, no guilt or shame. And then you have to ask what happened? How did this person move from point A to point B? Where did the wires cross or short out? Where could a person's intervention have made a difference? It's all hypothetical, and even if you are able to tap into some form of an explanation—the child was never loved, he was abused, teased without mercy—it doesn't excuse the behavior. But what it does is it brings all possibilities close enough that one cannot easily cast judgment without examining himself and those around him. The psychological undercurrents are what make each case unique while also opening it up in a way with which we can all identify some aspect.

The tragic story of Gary Gilmore, and that of the devastation he brought to his own family and those of his victims, was brilliantly brought to life in Norman Mailer's *The Executioner's Song*. However, the first time I picked up Mailer's book, I was unable to recognize its power. I had just finished reading *Shot in the Heart* and found Mailer's telling to be flat and emotionless. This, of course, is not true, and that book, along with the hours of interviews Mailer used, were of tremendous help to Mikal Gilmore. He expressed his gratitude to Mailer for uncovering truths about his family that he otherwise would never have known. *The Executioner's Song* is a powerful account, and the portrait of Gary Gilmore that emerges captures all the conflicts and complexities of an unloved, abused boy who grows into an angry, spiteful man with no social conscience. But what is missing is the ongoing voice in the background—the voice of the one left behind to live in the wake of the tragedy. As horrifying as the story of Gary Gilmore is, it is intensified in *Shot in the Heart* by the voice of someone whose life is forever connected to those tragic circumstances, but who has attempted to make up for a legacy of ruin.

On his last visit with his brother, Mikal Gilmore asked what his brother would have done had he made it to Portland (he was arrested on his way to the airport):

"Please, I have to know . . . would you have come to see me? . . ."

He [Gary] sighed and looked straight at me, and for a moment his eyes flashed an old anger. "And what would you have done if I had come to you?" he asked. "If I had come and said I was in trouble and needed help, needed a place to stay? Would you have taken me in? Would you have hidden me?"

I couldn't reply. The question had been turned back on me, and suddenly I could not stand the awfulness of my own answers. Gary sat there for long moments, holding me with his eyes, then said steadily: "I think I was coming to kill you. I think that's what would have happened. There simply may have been no other choice for you and no choice for me." His eyes softened and he gave me a tender smile. It was filled with the sad brokenness of our common history. "Do you understand why?" he asked.

I nodded back. Of course I understood why. I had escaped the family or at least thought I had. Gary had not . . . Oddly though, I also felt closer to Gary in that moment than I'd ever felt before. For just that second, I understood completely why he wanted to die.

This kind of moment pulls so many emotions to the surface at once—sadness, fear, compassion, relief. It expresses something so complex, we marvel at its existence, just as we do occurrences in nature. Because out of that chaos of complicated feelings and situations emerges a quiet, simple truth that has the power to alter the way we see the world by adding new dimensions of intellectual and emotional understanding. I think the orchestration of such an extraordinary phenomenon is beautiful. And, personally, that is all I need to know.

CHARLES FRAZIER

The Most Tempting Book I Read
THE TARAHUMARA by Antonin Artaud

One summer morning eight or ten years ago I walked down the street of a small town in the northern Mexico canyon country. The day was chilly and there had been rain during the night and the sky was all one color of gray. The streets were gray mud, and logging trucks ground through town in low gear, zagging to miss potholes. Many of the shop buildings were made of peeled logs. I walked past them looking for a restaurant or a grocery, but everything was closed, maybe due to some holiday of which I was ignorant. I stopped a couple of people and tried to ask when the shops would reopen, but the little bit of Spanish I know was learned in Peru and Bolivia, and it didn't seem to work at all here. I walked to the deserted plaza and took off my backpack and sat on a bench. The place

....

Charles Frazier lives in North Carolina and Florida. He has published one novel, *Cold Mountain*, which earned the National Book Award for Fiction in 1997.

seemed to be in the process of destruction or revision, a bulldozed roil of rocks and broken concrete and bare dirt.

For this I'd come nearly twenty-five-hundred miles overland from North Carolina—by car to El Paso and then by train, bus, thumb, and foot from there. It was a foolish trip, perhaps more than a little dangerous alone. But if someone from the town had walked up and asked why, out of all the places in the world, I had chosen to spend the better part of a week getting precisely here rather than, say, to a lavish resort hotel in the South Pacific with live dolphins in the swimming pool, I would at least have had an answer, however feeble. It involved a book I had read a few weeks earlier.

At that time I still taught English, and I used to take the weekly compositions from my freshman classes to one of the upper floors of the library with every intention of buckling down for the afternoon and reducing the stack by at least an inch before I drove home. I would find a table near the windows on the western side of the building and sit facing away from the shelves of books to admire the view. Then out with the red Bic and on with the job. Comma splices and vague thesis statements and weak logic noted, ideas for revision suggested until the margins were thick with scribble. I would grade a few, and then look out the window, and it was often at those moments that the pull of all those books around me would become too strong to resist, too tempting. Once I was out of the chair it was all over for freshman comp. I would prowl the stacks until I found something to read, preferably a book thin enough to finish in a single sitting—a book on Inca astronomy, Turgenev's *Diary of a Superfluous Man*, a biography of Crazy Horse. One afternoon in late winter I pulled from its slot a slender, dirty-blond book, a translation of *The Tarahumara* by Antonin Artaud, a French poet, dramatist, essayist, silent film actor, laudanum addict, and mental patient. I read it in one gulp. Even pausing to copy a few of the best sentences into my notebook, it took maybe an hour. *The Tarahumara* is an astonishing, mad, obsessive book, a fierce attempt by a man whose life is in a desperate place to make himself right, to fix himself after a life of breakage. It is based on a trip Artaud took in the mid-1930s, and he worked at the book for the rest of his life, which perhaps accounts for the odd relations among its parts. Some chapters were written fresh in Mexico, others later in the Rodez sanitarium where Artaud underwent a long series of electroshock treatments; the final chapter was completed in Paris only a few weeks before his death in 1948.

After the failure of his play, *Les Cenci,* in 1935, Artaud retreated from Paris and western civilization, which he found sick and held responsible for his own illness. Declaring that he wanted "to make contact with the Red Earth," he set out for Mexico. Much of *The Tarahumara* reflects this Romantic search for a primal culture, a primal experience. Here, for example, is the third paragraph: "Incredible as it may seem, the Tarahumara Indians live as if they were already dead. They do not see reality and they draw magical powers from the contempt they have for civilization." Well, all right, I'll admit that on the one hand I recognize Noble Savage hoodoo when I see it, whether it is in D. H. Lawrence or *Dances with Wolves.* But on the other hand, I very much wanted to go to a place with such inhabitants as Artaud describes.

Along with this native business, there is a great deal of *The Tarahumara* that is prototypic of Carlos Castaneda as well, since, once in the Sierra, Artaud fell in with a gang of peyote priests and developed a great attachment to their drug rites. He found the ceremonies dramatic in a way that corresponded closely with his proposals for the theater—the ritualistic, collective elements of it, the movement, music, sound, light that he had proposed in *The Theater and Its Double.* The drugs, though, were not one of the elements that much attracted me to the book. I suppose peyote was a pretty exotic thing for a Parisian in the thirties, but it held scant romance for me since the little wizened pellets seemed about as common as red clay when I was in school at Chapel Hill in the late sixties and early seventies.

Rather it was Artaud's dense, blinding vision of the landscape of northern Mexico's canyon lands that tempted me to go there, his hallucinatory reading of the terrain. In the book's brilliant second chapter, "The Mountain of Signs," he describes a living landscape haunted by a kind of symbolic discourse between man and nature. For nature's part of the conversation, what Artaud seems to have seen was the equivalent of going to Watauga County and finding not one Grandfather Mountain, but dozens of variations of the bearded figure in the rock. As he describes it, "The land of the Tarahumara is full of signs, forms, and natural effigies which in no way seem the result of chance—as if the gods themselves, whom one feels everywhere here, had chosen to express their powers by means of these strange signatures in which the figure of man is hunted down from all sides." To travel through such a charged space as Artaud describes would be rather like receiving a message in the form of images flashed before you in significant patterns of repetition and variation.

In response to this natural language of images, the Tarahumara have spoken back in kind. Artaud writes, "This inhabited Sierra, this Sierra which exhales a metaphysical thinking in its rocks, the Tarahumara have covered with signs, signs that are completely conscious, intelligent, and purposeful." Among these man-made notations on the land, I was most interested in the Tarahumara practice of marking important spots—passes through the mountains and the like—with rock cairns created by passers adding stone after stone over long periods of time. Cairn-building, Artaud writes, "is not a superstition but a technique of awareness. This means: Mark the point. Take note. Be aware of the contrary forces of life, for without this awareness you are dead."

I've added stones to similar cairns along pilgrimage routes up mountains in the west of Ireland and at fourteen-thousand foot passes in the Andean backcountry. In the Andes such constructs are called *apacheta*, and some of them are enormous—ten feet tall or more and forty or fifty feet in diameter, containing hundreds of thousands of stones added pilgrim by pilgrim for many hundreds of years. According to the early settlers of the southern Appalachians, the Cherokee or their predecessors constructed similar cairns at the gaps, the high points of paths through the mountains. As far as I know, not one remains intact, though at least a stone fish weir is still visible in the Little Tennessee River during drought times. The world's remaining cairns, those few still growing, are in a sense living things. To walk the old routes now and add stones to the cairns is to feed them and keep them alive. After reading Artaud, I wanted to go there and do that. So, though in general it seems to me that books ought to tempt their readers to think and feel seriously about their matter rather than seduce them into action, nevertheless, shortly after the semester ended, I set out for the Copper Canyon.

It is impossible to tell from *The Tarahumara* exactly what Artaud's route was; it is not that kind of travel book. And, anyway, I had no desire to re-create his trip. I just studied maps and plotted out a backcountry walk that looked to be the length I like to do alone. On the first day I left that muddy town with its bombed-out plaza and within an hour I was walking down a small canyon. The ochre walls were like facing rows of Easter Island heads. The grass in the valley floor between them was deep green from a long stretch of wet weather. Goats and cattle grazed all around, and up ahead I saw a small group of people sitting in a circle. I heard laughter and then fiddle music. The body of the fiddle was made from a cigar box, and its tone was about as you'd expect. As I neared them I raised a hand in greeting, but no one looked up. Later I walked past homesteads of log cabins and log corrals for the animals, and cornfields off to the side. Horsemen passed by. Beside the trail were mushroom-shaped rocks and head-shaped rocks, balancing rocks, caves, and overhangs grimed with old campfire smoke.

The farther I walked from town, the more the Tarahumara acted as if I wasn't there. If I stopped on the trail and asked directions, they kept walking. Sometimes I would see them approaching through the trees in fairly open country, very visible in their red headbands and white smocks. Next thing, they'd just be gone. I'd look for side trails they might have taken. None. I'd look behind rocks and tree trunks. Nothing. Awaiting further evidence, I worked on the assumption they knew how to disappear.

After a couple of days of this sort of benign pastoral walking I got seriously lost trying to find the valley of the Rio Tararecua. My maps were inadequate and trails tangled about every which way, as they tend to do in roadless inhabited areas. I remember taking a suspicious turn onto a white trail climbing through standing stones and cliff walls toward a pass. A large hawk stood at the edge of the cliff top. He spread his wings but did not fly. He watched me climb, turning slightly to keep addressing me as I progressed. When I reached the high point, it was marked with crosses and a small rock cairn. I added a stone, and the hawk stepped off the edge and looped down into the canyon and then caught a thermal and began gyring up in the rising air.

The next thing I remember from that day is bushwacking through dense pine woods for a while, which is the stage in getting lost where you have to admit that things are not going at all well. I eventually came out on a Tarahumara settlement where, again, no one seemed to want to acknowledge my existence except for a caramel-colored goat. It followed me as I went from cabin to cabin and tried to ask directions. I would talk and people just kept on hoeing. This was rather a different experience from coming into a very remote town in the Ecuadorean highlands and having school let out to celebrate your arrival and to admire your shiny Gore-Tex running suit. I think, all in all, I prefer the austere Tarahumara response. It says, "You really shouldn't be here. This place does not exist for your entertainment." I expect if some outlander fool had come wandering over the ridge onto my great-grandfather's farm in the North Carolina mountains asking the way to Asheville, the treatment the traveler received might have fallen some degree short of the last word in hospitality as well.

I gave up on communication and left the settlement on the trail that seemed to me, for no particular reason, most likely to go somewhere. Eventually it did. It emptied itself onto a dirt road that I walked for miles without passing a house and without a vehicle passing me. I came at last to a beautiful rancho, out in the middle of nowhere—lush corn, donkeys, goats, horses, cows, chickens. I stood at the gate and the master of the place came down and talked to me. He was a trim old gentleman with color in his cheeks and a sense of style in the way he wore his red bandanna loose about his neck and his clean straw hat tilted at a sporting angle. He said it was many hours walking to any place I knew the name of. It seemed to sadden him to have to tell me that news. He shook his head and looked at the ground.

I headed on up the road, and in an hour a truck loaded with big corrugated pipes stopped to give me a lift to town. I rode in back, standing on the shifting pipe and holding on to a length of chain as the truck banked into the turns. The Beach Boys song "Surfin' Safari" sprang to mind. The road wound along the canyon rim, and from my high vantage the vista was a long one, ridges and gorges charged with light all the way to the hazy edge of earth. Just a little slice of it was the entirety of my walk.

Not far from town, the truck stopped briefly, and I took out my camera and snapped a photograph of this long view, thinking it might capture something of Artaud's meaning when he wrote in *The Tarahumara* that "when one climbs until one can see around one a vast circle of peaks, one can no longer doubt that one has arrived at one of those sensitive points on the earth where life has shown her first effect." Clunky translation aside, finding such a place is pretty much what tempted me away from home to begin with. But looking at the somewhat faded photo these years later, the image is utterly bland—just low pine hills, dusty rocks—a weak artifact of a trip that confirmed for me Artaud's insistence that awareness is all we have. As he puts it, "To the Tarahumara, there is no sin: evil is loss of consciousness."

ELIZABETH HAY

The Most Fearless Book I Read

5001 NIGHTS AT THE MOVIES by Pauline Kael

Even voracious readers can go off books. It happens suddenly. You hit a wall and find yourself unable to take pleasure in any book at all. It is the clearest sign I know of being down in the dumps.

In 1989, my husband and I were living in a dark, narrow, first-floor walk-through in upper Manhattan with our two tiny children who didn't sleep. I think it's fair to say that, in a manner familiar to many new parents, I was losing my mind. In those days I would open a book and the words would bounce against my eyes like gravel against a windshield. Fiction especially had this effect. I was trying to write fiction, yet I couldn't stomach the artifice, concoction, and preening length of the

. . . .

Elizabeth Hay's two novels are *Garbo Laughs* and *A Student of Weather*. Her most recent story collection is *Small Change*. In 2002 she won the Marian Engel Award for her body of work. She lives in Ottawa, Canada.

novels I picked up. So far gone was I that I couldn't even understand what "fiction" meant, and in truth I hated the word.

To alleviate our tied-down circumstances, we bought a VCR and set it up at the halfway point of our long dark spaghetti strand of an apartment. On the other side of the VCR were the pigeons in the air shaft, and beyond the pigeons, five feet away, the peeling wall of an abandoned building. As it turned out, however, half a block away lay Shangri-la. On the first floor of another five-story walk-up, filling shelves that reached from wooden floor to high ceiling, were thousands of movies encased in black boxes. It looked almost like a library, and was probably the best video store in the city. At the far end, in a sort of Rolodex bin, were the covers of all the movie musicals ever made. Every weekend, I made a beeline for this bin. In my childhood, you have to understand, we didn't have a television and few movies were allowed. My father was a high school principal, puritanical by nature, and my mother a rationer by bent. I had a lot of catching up to do.

And so began our movie education. At the ages of two, four, and thirty-eight respectively, my son, my daughter, and I began to watch Fred Astaire and Ginger Rogers, Gene Kelly and Judy Garland, and Cary Grant, Cary Grant, Cary Grant. Awash in guilty love, my finger glued to the rewind button, I reminded myself of the blue-rinse ladies who used to sidle up to the sour-faced librarian in my childhood and get the Harlequin romances she saved for them alone. Not that I had sunk that low. I wasn't reading Harlequins, just movie star biographies. Saturday mornings, while my daughter hopped around in preballet at the 63rd Street Y, I haunted the movie stacks of the public library at Lincoln Center, secretly thumbing through bad books about Hollywood, more ashamed of myself by the minute, and wrestling with the fundamental literary question: Why are books about movie stars so boring?

I wanted nothing more than to make the movies last, to extend their two-hour intensity into the rest of my life. But the sad truth is that after the movies ended, I felt emptier than ever. My children and I became all too accustomed to the peevish aftermath of movie musicals. What was I to do? In a pinch I had always turned to books. But they were still failing me.

Then one cold day, in the fall of the year, I came upon the writings of Pauline Kael. Her essay "The Man from Dream City" caught my eye, and within seconds I was beside myself with joy. A smart woman with a sharp tongue and a way with words understood my infatuation with Cary Grant and shared it. Here was a woman with the courage of her romantic convictions. A writer who knew how to take the vividness on the screen and continue it on the page.

Her *5001 Nights at the Movies* is a four-inch-thick volume of thumbnail reviews, blazingly honest and fearless with a particular kind of jazzy fearlessness. On *Notorious*: "Will suspicious, passive Grant succeed in making Bergman seduce him, or will he take over?" On *Casablanca*: "Ingrid Bergman became a popular favorite when Humphrey Bogart, as Rick, the most famous saloonkeeper in screen history, treated her like a whore." On Michael Douglas in *Romancing the Stone*: "His face exaggerates everything and registers nothing." On Barbra Streisand in *Funny Lady*: she's "no longer human; she's like a bitchy female impersonator imitating Barbra Streisand."

What hooked me was that she both condoned my addiction and mocked it, her passionate ambivalence in tune with my own temperament. I didn't want to have my cake and eat it, too, I wanted to have my cake and spit out the frosting. Open the book to any of its nearly nine hundred pages and you have, nailed down, what makes a movie work. She examined—and this is very exciting for anyone who wants to make something, whether it's a story, or a novel, or anything else—she examined what made a performance fail or succeed, a movie resonate or peter out, and it was often dishonesty that doomed an actor or a movie, a grossieagerness either to please or to impress. I read her reviews with an eye to my own failings.

Movies were something she knew from beginning to end, from the silents through the talkies to World War II, the Cold War, Vietnam, and since, Hollywood and elsewhere. Born in 1919 and "blessed with movie-loving parents," her life paralleled the life of the movies and she was an enthusiast from the beginning. She was also a great reader who studied philosophy, then held a number of jobs before she began reviewing movies when she was thirty-five. When I read her, I felt I was being led by a mature observer through the highs and lows of life. I was being guided by a good writer with a real eye for fakery and bullshit, especially poetic bullshit. No doubt her fearlessness took strength from the cowardice that washed through so much of the industry. Her greatest scorn she reserved for the moneymen, her greatest sympathy for the unselfconscious risk takers, the natural actors, the transparent directors, who threw themselves into their work, no holds barred. Read everything she's written about Robert Altman, for instance, not just the capsule summaries in *5001 Nights* but the full reviews published in her volumes of collected writings available in libraries, and you have a portrait of an unpredictable, innovative, unevenly successful director who "has what Joyce had: a love of the supreme juices of everyday life."

She provides a portrait set within the framework of a whole century of movies, history, popular taste. What she gives you is a sense of continuity. I learned about silent stars Harry Langdon, Buster Keaton, Harold Lloyd—how they were viewed at the time, how they stand up now. I found out why Bette Davis's performance in *The Little Foxes* wasn't as good as Tallulah Bankhead's on stage, but why Tallulah, for all her greatness, didn't translate from stage to screen. I read about movies I would never bother to see, because what she said was useful and interesting. In fact, that fall I read nothing else. I remember lying on my bed in the dim light of our narrow apartment, entranced with her ability to react. There was nothing passive about the way she watched movies. Nothing artificial about her direct and urgent style.

Here's *The Stripper*, made in 1963, a movie she describes as having "the dreary, liberal Freudian Sunday School neatness of second-rate serious drama," but with a performance by Joanne Woodward that's worth watching since "she gives the Marilyn Monroe-ish role a nervousness that cuts through its pathos." I make a mental note to avoid moral neatness, especially dreary liberal Freudian neatness, and give more thought to Joanne Woodward than I otherwise would have, and I continue reading. Here's *Sunrise*, "a near masterpiece" made in 1927 by "the great German director F. W. Murnau," and with "some masterly sequences: the seduction under a full moon, the wife's flight (she boards a trolley)," and I see that I've underlined these words in pencil to remind myself to think about scenes, especially—why bother with anything else?—scenes of seduction and flight. Here's *The Sundowners* from 1960, "a large, episodic movie with a strong emotional texture," and good performances by Robert Mitchum and Deborah Kerr, of whom I'm very fond, and I've circled it, though I still haven't seen it and probably never will. For years I've read this book with a pencil because I'm a writer looking for clues about form, character, dramatic shape, and momentum, and because I'm a movie lover with a huge appetite for movie love.

How interesting it is to follow an honest temperament. She falls in love. She gossips. She recoils. She loses her temper. Reaction, intensity, insight. She doesn't shy away from her reactions, she isn't embarrassed by them, and as a result the quality of her analysis doesn't flag. There seems to be no limit to the play between sympathetic and critical understanding in her reviews, nothing that can't be thought about in an interesting way.

As a hardworking writer who produced week after week, writing in longhand at a drafting table and often through the night, she managed to turn even the worst movie to account, using it to write about the larger world. She was not a snob. She loved movies not "film." She defended *Charade,* made in 1963 with Cary Grant and Audrey Hepburn and widely panned by the press, as "a debonair macabre thriller—romantic, scary, satisfying," indeed, one of the most satisfying movies in a year when entertaining movies were not the trend.

We shared the same taste in men. She loved Sean Connery and Gene Kelly and Cary Grant and Jeff Bridges and Peter O'Toole, too. And because, in my dark apartment, itself like a tiny arts cinema, I was having lavish love affairs with these men, rewinding movies to watch, yet again, the look on Cary Grant's face when he realized that Eva Marie Saint was not a tramp but a secret agent, or that Claude Rains and his evil mother were actually poisoning Ingrid Bergman, I needed somebody to reassure me that, though I was certainly going to the dogs, I wasn't a complete lunatic. She gave me license to love without apology. She blew away the snobbish restrictions that curtailed my childhood. She allowed for honest love and honest dislike. It takes a long time, a lifetime, for some of us to dislike without apology. There is an art to disliking, just as there's an art to loving. Pauline Kael might write off a movie, she often wrote off a movie, but she didn't write off her love of the movies. She was the queen of anti-Puritans.

Here's a confession. I often got lost in *5001 Nights* to the detriment of everything else. I would be at my desk, boring myself with some current piece of writing, when a movie would float through my mind and I would get up, locate her on the shelf, sit down on the side of the bed and not stir for an hour. I would look up Sean Connery in the index, and read every entry. Or Paul Newman. Or

Cary Grant, once again. It was like eating chocolates on a treadmill; since she was tough. I had to read both pleasant and unpleasant things about these lovely men, and why they were effective in one movie and not another. But we agreed about enough. If I had more time for *Guys and Dolls* than she had, she had plenty of time for Marlon Brando.

It will come as no surprise that I'm writing a novel about movies and that Pauline Kael is in it. I've relaxed a bit since those tormented days of mad motherhood. The word "fiction" doesn't scare me the way it used to. Now I see it less as an insurmountable wall than an old corset, well used and expansive, that can hold just about anything. In the novel, one of the characters, caught in a tug-of-war between real love and movie love, writes letters to Pauline Kael that she never mails. These moments in an ongoing, one-sided correspondence are the most pleasurable for me to write. I like being in her company. She keeps me connected to the past and steadies me as I move ahead in the story, an ideal character, in other words.

My copy of *5001 Nights* is held together by an elastic band, since I'm no longer the only one who paws through it. My gangly, careless, movie-fanatic son, now thirteen years old, can't believe that Pauline Kael didn't like *West Side Story*. He's outraged that she found fault with *Guys and Dolls* but mollified by her ardent enthusiasm for *Nashville* and *The Godfather* and *The Letter*. He is unlikely to ever see the book the way I do, as a sweeping history of movies and movie watching, a grand, untiring book that holds within it a lifetime of observations on a heroic scale. But at least he knows who she is. I watch with some concern as he carts it off to his bedroom. Be careful, I say. That book is important to me.

AIMEE BENDER

The Most Intuitive Book I Read
THE WIND-UP BIRD CHRONICLE by Haruki Murakami

I began Haruki Murakami's 1997 novel, *The Wind-Up Bird Chronicle*, on an airplane; it seemed interesting enough, and the prose was readable and unassuming. I was airplane tired and I didn't want a book that would ask for too much from me right then in terms of sentence-level complexity, and I'd heard good things about it from a reliable friend. I was reading along, enjoying the odd turns of events, when about a hundred pages in I hit upon a scene of violence I found so gruesome and upsetting I could hardly touch the pages. Suddenly, smack in the middle of the story line about a young unemployed man eating sandwiches, there's a retelling of a soldier being skinned alive in Outer Mongolia during World War II. When I looked back later, I was amazed to discover that the scene was only a

....

Aimee Bender is the author of a collection of short stories, *The Girl in the Flammable Skirt,* and a novel, *An Invisible Sign of My Own*. Her fiction has been published in *Granta, GQ, Harper's,* the *Paris Review,* and other journals. She teaches creative writing at the University of Southern California.

couple of pages; at the time, it felt like it went on and on forever. The following day, I asked my book recommender friend if there were other such grisly surprises; this is rare for me—I don't usually like to know anything about what's ahead. But Murakami could go anywhere now with his novel. I had to follow him blindly, and it left me both shaken and compelled.

After I finished the novel, I thought about it for weeks, months. It did not slip out of my mind. It gained richness and complexity in my memory the more I lived with it. Plotwise, it's not so easy to summarize: It's something of an epic about an unemployed man who goes on a surreal journey when his wife disappears one afternoon, while at the same time, through monologues and flashbacks, it addresses Japan's role in World War II. This is a big and sloppy book, and two-thirds in, the narrator basically vanishes for a while, to the reader's annoyance, and there are countless inexplicable characters whose actions I never really understand. Just when my interest in someone is piqued, they leave. Murakami writes like a mystery novelist—he's apparently a fan of Raymond Chandler—but he doesn't solve much and even those few answers are still pretty open ended.

He is also a fan of jazz, and if jazz and mysteries could merge, they would probably look a lot like Murakami's plot progression. If a reader is looking for completion, then this is a highly frustrating book. I've read it three times now, and it unfolds itself more each time, but still, there are movements and twists that I can't quite pin down. But I don't mind a bit. I really could give a flying hoot. Because what he teaches me is on every page, regardless of what happens. With Murakami, there's something extremely present in his sentences; he's right there in the story, struggling through it with us, so completely intuitively focused, and I think it's the force of this intent that makes me believe in him completely. Nothing is imposed. It is a pathway formed simply by the utter commitment Murakami has to his own process.

There's a story my mother tells of when she saw Martha Graham perform for the first time. She was thirty then, and she'd spent her childhood taking loads of ballet classes, tondue-ing and tour-jete-ing her way through high school and college. In 1970, bull-dozed by hype, she got student tickets for Graham's company at UCLA's Royce Hall, and for three nights in a row, she settled herself in the balcony and watched the performances. But what was all the fuss about? She wasn't impressed.

On the night of the final performance, she spied a free seat in the front row, and wanting a change of viewpoint, she crept down the stairs and grabbed it, never once suspecting that the evening ahead would actually change her brain. The performance that night was *Clytemnestra,* and the lead dancer was Graham herself. And, even at sixty years old (maybe in part because of it) Graham's per-formance as a woman bound in a terrifying dilemma chilled my mother to the core. This was no decorative prettiness. This was no buoyant pink satin. The movement had a fluidity that defied the orderly nature of ballet rules, and an unpredictability that matched the character's experience. Who knew which way Graham's body would move next. My mother was on the absolute edge of her seat. Never in her life had she, a fan of classical ballet, felt the gut-level power of dance like this before. Afterward, she said she did not eat or sleep for two days. She was so utterly nourished and invigorated by what she had seen, she did not need to.

I was always envious of that story, because it seemed so won-derfully dramatic—she did not even eat? I, perpetually hungry, could not imagine it. But I understand better, year by year, the feeling she had. The moment where the learning curve goes off the charts. It's the opposite of memorizing dates in history class, hoping against hope that the facts will stick; some performances or books or films or lessons, through their rule breaking, teach their audience all at once. I think this is my favorite thing that a piece of art can do: reduce me to some kind of preverbal state of sustenance and learning. But it's rare to come by.

Like Graham, Murakami's sense of movement is less about perfect turns and plot twists, and more about somehow getting inside the depth of the human body and experience, and revealing it from the inside out. This shift in priorities makes space for intuition, and Murakami's inner voice, guiding him from one scene to the next, is a well-honed muscle. To sustain the motion of the story, he brings in everything he can: surrealism, psychology, history, sociology, and a bizarre and wonderful variety of character voices. It's a big story, and he knows it, and it's clear that it takes great concentration to write it. In an interview on Salon.com, Murakami said he must take care of himself physically to gear up to write. It's so demanding a process that he has to remember to exercise and eat well so that he can retain the focus and capacity he needs to move with the story.

So there is Murakami: choreographing for himself, keeping the body as alert as possible so he can attend to the shifts and expansions of the mind. Perhaps this accounts somewhat for the physical feeling to his storytelling. The landscapes are dreamlike, but the people are all flesh and blood: They eat constantly, they have sex, albeit in unusual ways, they climb into the setting and interact, physically, with both the tangible and the intangible.

Because of what I feel to be an overwhelmingly deep attention to this method of telling a story, I don't have any investment in the outcome of Murakami's plot. I'm just interested in seeing what choices he makes. I relinquish my own wishes for the book entirely to his, and in that moment, he becomes the best kind of teacher.

Often when I love books this much, I feel possessive of them and pretend the writer and I have some special bond. In the worst-case scenarios, I get jealous and petty when other people say they love the book, too. But for some inexplicable reason, with Murakami, I feel like there's enough to go around. He promotes sharing. He can have special bonds with everyone, for God's sake. I love teaching this book, because although there's plenty to talk about, it seems to evade any destructive deconstruction. In part, I think this is because the book does not add up at all; I'm not worried that someone will waltz in and reduce his work to an articulate pea. And the complaints people have about *The Wind-Up Bird Chronicle* are often what I love the most—its messiness, its hanging threads, its matter-of-fact surrealism. But I wonder, too, if Murakami's faith in his own process, his own patient listening, rubs off on the reader. He does not seem creatively worried. This book is not supposed to be the end-all, be-all; it's the end-some, be-some instead, and that cuts into my petty possessive instincts. He's tapping into the large mysterious fields of his mind and his country, and all of us are welcome to come walk around in them, and then go off and walk around in our own.

One of my favorite moments in the novel is one of the quietest. The narrator, Toru, is at a turning point in his journey, but there's nothing to turn to. He has no idea what to do next. His wife is gone. He has met psychics, war soldiers, phone-sex callers, politicians, teenagers, and businessmen. All his leads are spent. So his uncle tells him that at times such as this, he likes to go and look at people's faces. Toru is nothing if not open minded, so he goes to downtown Tokyo, and for several pages, Murakami tells us calmly about his lead character sitting down and looking at people, waiting for something to happen.

The writing is simple and direct. It seems reasonable to figure that Murakami himself was doing the same; he was waiting for his novel to tell him where to go next. Most authors cut this step—it's likely that they are doing it, but in the final draft, they won't show their waiting time. But Murakami does not edit his process for his readers here. His process is our process is Toru's process. Toru does eventually meet someone, but nothing happens for a while; instead, through the small details revealed inside the pages, enough has gently shifted in the narrative for Murakami to take us to the next place. The fact that he, as a writer, insisted on including this passage is intensely calming to me. I am interested the entire time Toru is looking at faces—another tangible, physical moment—even though it's certainly a less exciting point of the plot. But Murakami is there, working, listening, and so am I.

What this does, for me, is create a rock-solid trust. I put my wholehearted readership into the intense focus of his listening. This is what I'm looking for, over and over, in books: when I reach the point where the writer can take all the time they want, make mistakes, spill all over the place—and I'm delighted. I'm living inside each sentence so deeply that wherever they guide me, I will follow with interest.

I can't speak for my mother, but my sense when she tells her Graham story is that what she felt that night was an amazing surrender to the movement she saw on the stage. She gave herself up to it. She trusted the dancer on the stage and the surprise and inevitability of every moment seeped inside her and became a permanent part of how she looked at the world. And although my experience with Murakami is not textured like my mother's with Graham, in that it was slower and thicker, and in a way, less immediate, I remain haunted by it. In its own patient way, the book crept into my brain, and it shows no signs of leaving.

MARGOT LIVESEY

The Most Scottish Book I Read
SUNSET SONG by Lewis Grassick Gibbon

Many Americans have never traveled to Scotland, but the tiny country seems vivid in their imaginations. It conjures images of kilts and heather and the poetry of Robert Burns. When I tell people that I grew up there, they frequently respond with questions about haggis and shortbread and which clan I belong to. I belong to the McEwen's but I'm not sure these days that we count as a clan and although haggis and shortbread played a role in my childhood it was all much more complicated than that. In fact, the ease with which outsiders define our nation is almost the exact opposite of the difficulty natives have in describing our national character and identity.

What does it mean to be Scottish?

The essential problem is that Scotland has, in one way or

. . . .

Margot Livesey grew up in Scotland and now divides her time between London and Boston. She has taught in several writing programs and is currently a writer in residence at Emerson College in Boston. Her novels include *Homework, Criminals,* and most recently *Eva Moves the Furniture.*

another, been subjugated to England for nearly four hundred years, a culture within a culture. This double consciousness, this confusion, was intensified for me because I grew up an outsider in several ways. My father taught mathematics and geography at Trinity College, a boys' public school (by which I mean private) that had been founded by the Victorian prime minister, William Gladstone, for the sons of clergymen. Gladstone's ambition was to keep these young men free from the ways of vice. With that in mind the school was ten slow miles from the nearest town, in a valley called Glenalmond on the edge of the Highlands. I knew every tree and stream and rock of those few square miles by heart. When I looked out of my bedroom window, I could see the old drove roads, used in the eighteenth century to bring the sheep and cattle down from the Highlands to the Lowland markets, scarring the hills.

Like the other great public schools, Eton and Harrow for example, Trinity College was, at this time, an almost entirely masculine environment. The notion of women teachers was still unthinkable during the 1960s and most of the masters were bachelors. My father became a rare exception when he married my mother, the school nurse. Of course, she had to give notice. In Bell's Cottage, the first house I remember, we had no fridge, no vacuum cleaner, no phone. Our one newfangled machine was a huge wireless, with stations as far away as Vienna and Budapest listed on the glowing green dial.

In addition to being thoroughly masculine and old fashioned, the school was thoroughly English. All the masters were graduates of Oxford or Cambridge, and many of the pupils came from south of the border or had been sent home to study by parents working abroad to keep the Empire afloat. As a girl there was no question of my attending, and I traveled the ten miles back and forth to Morrison's Academy for Girls—another remarkably English institution. Edinburgh used to be known as the Athens of the north, and education throughout Scotland had a reputation for rigor and excellence but in the 1960s we studied neither the history, nor the geography, of our native land. Instead we learned about the repeal of the Corn Laws and the French Revolution and drew pictures of Norwegian fjords and the Nile Delta. Except for a few poems by Robert Burns, the only work of literature we read that concerned Scotland was *Macbeth*, and that was more to do with the author than the subject matter. Indeed the only aspect of local culture I remember studying was Scottish country dancing. At the compulsory school Christmas dance we were expected to do the Gay Gordons and the more complicated Dashing White Seargent without putting a foot wrong.

All of this, along with the vagaries of literary reputation, goes some way to explain why I did not read Lewis Grassic Gibbon's 1932 novel *Sunset Song* until I was nearly thirty. I recognized the book instantly, at some deep level, as embodying the essence of my homeland. Here was that commingling of hardship and beauty that I saw as I journeyed back and forth to school. Here were the people I glimpsed when I talked to the local farmers about their childhoods. By the time I read the novel, I was already living in America, and part of what I recognized in Grassic Gibbon's intense, lyrical evocation of place and person was the exile's longing.

Lewis Grassic Gibbon was born James Leslie Mitchell in 1901 and grew up in the north east of Scotland, not far from the city of Aberdeen. After spending six years as a clerk in the RAF, he settled outside London and became a full-time writer in 1929. During his short life he wrote prolifically, both novels and nonfiction. He adopted his pen name, appropriately enough his mother's name, for his trilogy *A Scots Quair*, of which *Sunset Song* is the first volume. I don't think it is only my imagination that all three novels are infused with a kind of urgency, as if Mitchell already knew that he would die of a perforated ulcer at the age of thirty-four, before he could revise the last volume.

Mitchell's life story is a very Scottish one, the rural childhood, the flight south for work, the early death—but not as Scottish as the radiant, heartfelt, heartbreaking, first volume of the trilogy. *Sunset Song* follows the early life of the spirited, clever, passionate Chris Guthrie who grows up the only daughter of a poor hill farmer in the settlement of Kinraddie. It also follows the life of that community in the years immediately prior to, during, and after the Great War.

Let me say, if I can, what makes the novel so intensely Scottish. Partly it is the voice for which Gibbon offers a mock apology at the beginning and in which, like his great ancestor Robert Louis Stevenson, he cunningly mixes Scots and English, so that even the most nervous English-speaking reader can follow him into the poetry of the Scottish tongue: "Now that was in summer, the time of fleas and glegs and golochs in the fields, when stirks would start up from the drowsy cud-chewing to wild and feckless racing, the glegs biting through hair and hide."

Partly it is the exquisite detail with which Gibbon describes the land and the many tasks of the small holder. He knows intimately the bone-breaking, relentless, unrewarding nature of farming and yet he also captures those rare mornings when the sun shines and the breeze blows softly and everything is green and fecund. It seems almost a commonplace to say of certain stories and novels that they capture the relationship between person and place, but *Sunset Song* actually does do this and does it so keenly that wherever you come from, whatever the landscape dear to your eyes, you will find, after you read the novel, that you now have another place in your imagination that you may visit when you choose. When the busy city streets and the malls shimmering with plastic make you weary then you may go to Kinraddie and climb up the hill at the back of Chris's farm to the group of standing stones beside the loch. When Chris decides, after the early death of her parents, to remain in Kinraddie rather than go south to become a teacher, we understand and even applaud her choice, though we know it will bring her heartbreak.

Partly it is the portrayal of the Guthrie family: the hot-tempered, dour, hardworking father; the sweet, blithe mother brought to childbed so often that she finally kills herself and her two youngest children; the clear-eyed, oldest son, Will, driven like so many others to emigrate. At the heart of the novel, though, is Chris Guthrie herself and the unfolding of her life as she goes from being a biddable girl to a strong-minded young woman who must make her own way in the world. But isn't this, after all, the familiar theme of *Jane Eyre* or *Anne of Green Gables* or even *The Portrait of a Lady*? Yes, but none of these heroines, I would argue, struggles with Chris's peculiarly Scottish fate: the burden of a double life.

This doubleness of life and soul has a long history in Scotland and her literature; perhaps it has something to do with the country being colonized, perhaps with the further schism between Lowlands and Highlands, between those who remained loyal to England and those who followed Bonnie Prince Charlie, between those who spoke pure Scots and those who adopted the English tongue, between those who stayed and those who left. It has its most famous embodiment in Robert Louis Stevenson's *The Strange Case of Dr. Jekyll and Mr. Hyde* in which Stevenson creates a man so divided in his nature and impulses that the two halves can never meet. Chris is no Jekyll and Hyde but the division between her two selves is profound and, at times, painful:

So that was Chris and her reading and schooling, two Chrisses there were that fought for her heart and tormented her. You hated the land and the coarse speak of the folk and learning was brave and fine one

day; and the next you'd waken with the peewits crying across the hills,
deep and deep, crying in the heart of you and the smell of the earth in
your face, almost you'd cry for that, the beauty of it and the sweetness
of the Scottish land and skies . . . And the next minute that passed
from you, you were English, back to the English words so sharp and
clean and true.

Throughout her life Chris wrestles with these two identities, choosing, as her author seems to have done, first one then the other. They make her life both richer and harder. And I would have to say the same about myself. Living as I do mostly in America, trying to conjure my native land onto the page, I feel I've taken both Chris and her creator's double lives one step further. Like Chris, I often wish I'd never heard of England, let alone the New World, but I also marvel at the great good fortune that allows me to go back, year after year, and see the landscape I love as if for the first time.

CLYDE EDGERTON

The Most Technically Elegant Book I Read

STICK AND RUDDER: AN EXPLANATION OF THE ART OF FLYING
by Wolfgang Langewiesche

I don't normally read technical stuff. But I've read many books, pamphlets, and manuals about airplanes and about flying airplanes. Much of this reading was assigned while I was an air force pilot—and student pilot—during the late sixties and early seventies, and included complicated formulas, charts, and graphs. And to explain how an airplane wing creates lift, there was always Bernoulli's Theorem. I carefully studied all my written assignments and managed about fifteen hundred hours of accident-free flying during my five-year military stint. I didn't crash—then.

After I separated from the air force in 1971, I kept flying airplanes—off and on—and reading about flying. I finally bought a 1946 Piper PA-12 Super Cruiser in 1989. I named her

....

Clyde Edgerton teaches creative writing at the University of North Carolina at Wilmington. He has published eight novels including *Raney, The Floatplane Notebooks, Where Trouble Sleeps,* and, most recently, *Lunch at the Piccadilly*.

Annabelle. She was beautiful—a red and white fabric-covered, old-fashioned, nose-high "taildragger." I have never been more attached to a possession. Just after my maiden flight in *Annabelle*, I read the most technically elegant book I've ever read, a book penned in 1944: *Stick and Rudder: An Explanation of the Art of Flying*, by Wolfgang Langewiesche.

And then in 1991, after two years of flying all over North Carolina, down to Mississippi, up to D.C., I reached the end of my honeymoon. I crashed *Annabelle*. She was totaled, but nobody was hurt. I crashed not because of *Stick and Rudder*, but in spite of it. In fact, *Stick and Rudder* helped save my life, but before I say how, I want you to know more about this technical book—this little work of art.

Most books about flying airplanes start something like this: "The primary objective of this chapter is to demonstrate to the reader the theory of flight through an overview of the four basic forces of flight: lift, drag, weight, and thrust." A detailed analysis of each force follows. The prose is dry, non-personal. Langewiesche begins: "Get rid at the outset of the idea that the airplane is only an air-going sort of automobile. It isn't. It may sound like one and smell like one, and it may have been interior-decorated to look like one: but the difference is—it goes on wings. And a wing is an odd thing, strangely behaved, hard to understand, tricky to handle." The language is refreshing, suspenseful, and accurate. After his opening paragraph, Langewiesche explains how a wing flies. But he doesn't explain à la air force technique—by way of Bernoulli's Theorem. He says, "When you studied theory of flight in ground school, you were probably taught a good deal of fancy stuff concerning an airplane's wing and just how it creates lift. Perhaps you remember Bernoulli's Theorem: how the air, in shooting around the long way over the top of the wing, has to speed up, and how in speeding up it drops some of its pressure, and how it hence exerts a suction on the top surface of the wing. Forget it. . . . The main fact of all heavier-than-air flight is this: The wing keeps the airplane up by pushing the air down. . . . Trying to understand the piloting of airplanes by concentrating on Bernoulli is like trying to catch on to tennis by studying just exactly how the rubber molecules behave in a tennis ball . . . instead of simply observing that it bounces!"

Langewiesche goes on to explain angle of attack (the angle at which the wing meets the air). The wing is like a hand out the window of a fast-moving car. The hand, level, goes neither up nor down. But move the front of your hand upward slightly (thus creating a "positive angle of attack") and you see how, at this positive angle of attack, your hand meets the air and washes it down, thus creating lift. Your hand moves up. This would hold true if the car were going up a hill or down a hill. An airplane wing keeps the airplane up by pushing the air down. Your hand is pushing against the wind at an angle and getting pushed back. Creating that slight positive angle of attack, i.e., raising the front of your level hand a bit, creates lift. All that is required is some sort of force to move the car forward. Think about rolling down the runway in a commercial jet. The engine's thrust is moving you forward. The wings are large hands out the windows, built into the aircraft at a slightly positive angle of attack so that, given faster and faster ground speed, those wings finally lift the whole aircraft up into the air.

Then it begins to get complicated, but *Stick and Rudder* gets it right. It is divided into seven parts. Here they are—basic, clear:

I.   *Wings*
II. *Some Air Sense*
III. *The Controls*

Many flying books would forgo number V above and would include separate sections on "The Landing Approach," "Final Approach," "The Touchdown," etc. I love the elegance of number V: "Getting Down."

And reading *Stick and Rudder*, I was able to clearly feel and see "the paradox of the glide." Let's say you're almost out of fuel and want to glide as far as possible. You pull back on your power and start a glide. Here's the paradox: By holding the nose up you "feel like" you're going to glide a long way, while the fact is that by pointing the nose down more steeply, you can glide farther. You must behave counterintuitively. By pointing the nose down more steeply you quickly gain speed, which allows greater lift than you'd have at slow speeds, therefore the airplane glides farther than if you held the nose up and thus slowed down. That way—holding the nose up—the resulting lack of speed and therefore lift on the wing causes a high sink rate and your distance over the ground will be relatively short. It's not that I didn't understand these principles while I was a pilot in the air force. Rather, I hadn't been able to "feel" conditions as I read about them. Reading *Stick and Rudder* put me in the cockpit—seeing, sensing, judging.

Ah-ha. The book was teaching me about writing, showing me how fancy, strange concepts can be made plain by a writer who is able to write clearly and simply—about technical stuff—by using relationships and sensations familiar to most of us. And not in a belittling or reductionist way. *Stick and Rudder*'s clever use of metaphor and lively, active sentences that sound like talk helped Mr.

Langewiesche do something he hadn't planned. As he went about explaining the art of flying and in the process making the unfamiliar familiar, he inspired me to be a better writer.

The crash. I crashed because I was stupid and because I was smart. The stupid part is this: I chose a bad day to fly. The wind was from the wrong direction and I took off with a high wind to my back. A no-no. Unfortunately, the short, grass runway was downhill and takeoffs were allowed in only the downhill direction (after starting the take-off roll around a dogleg). The smart part was that after becoming airborne, I immediately put the aircraft back on the ground, straight ahead. I put it down on the remaining runway, rolled into a field, hit a ditch, and flipped *Annabelle* over onto her top. I put it back down because I felt that if I continued I might not make it over a line of trees ahead in the distance. I put it down straight ahead because of all that had been eloquently (and at length) preached and demonstrated to me in *Stick and Rudder:* Don't attempt low, slow turns.

Langewiesche's re-creation of sensation through clarity, simplicity, and sensible use of language had helped me get into my bones, while reading, what had been in my head about the extreme danger of low, slow flying.

I haven't flown an airplane since the crash. But I plan to. In the meantime, *Stick and Rudder: An Explanation of the Art of Flying* remains close at hand. And when I get lonesome for some flying, I start reading. On any page. It puts me in the air.

PETER CAMERON

The Queerest Book I Read

THE SCAPEGOAT by Jocelyn Brooke

"Queer" is one of those slippery words that means different things to different people, different things at different times. My dictionary (*Webster's*) offers these several definitions: Differing in some odd way from what is usual or normal: ECCENTRIC, UNCONVENTIONAL; mildly insane: TOUCHED; absorbed or interested to an extreme or unreasonable degree: OBSESSED; sexually deviate: HOMOSEXUAL. Like many words with multiple meanings, queer is usually used according to one of its definitions—it's difficult to think of something queer in every sense of the word. Difficult, that is, until you have read *The Scapegoat*.

Several years ago Turtle Point Press began republishing "lost" books with introductions by contemporary authors. I was asked to write about *The Scapegoat* by Jocelyn Brooke (in this

. . . .

Peter Cameron lives in New York City. He is the author of *The Half You Don't Know: Selected Stories* and four novels: *Leap Year, The Weekend, Andorra,* and *The City of Your Final Destination*.

case, Jocelyn is a man), a short novel originally published by The Bodley Head, a British publisher, in 1948. It is the exceedingly curious and macabre story, set in rural England during World War II, of an orphaned thirteen-year-old boy, Duncan, who comes to live with his bachelor uncle, Gerald March. Duncan is delicate, nervous, and effeminate; Gerald, a former soldier-turned-gentleman farmer, is strong, robust, and almost preternaturally masculine. The uncle attempts to "make a man" out of his nephew, forcing him to take cold baths, join in early-morning naked calisthenics, and learn to ride and shoot, but his efforts are met with resistance and failure. Duncan and Gerald are weirdly paralyzed by their mutual sexual attraction, and their menage ends tragically. After spending a chaste night in bed together, Gerald beats his nephew to death (mildly insane: TOUCHED).

I can think of only a few books whose entire cast of characters is of the same gender, excepting those books about soldiers, or cowboys, or girls at boarding schools, and usually even in these books there is a token character representing the "opposite" sex, to add some relief, or throw into relief, the overwhelmingly masculine or feminine world. But there are no women in *The Scapegoat* (differing in some odd way from what is usual or normal: ECCENTRIC, UNCONVENTIONAL). Duncan's mother dies before the book begins and is never remembered with any specificity. Gerald mentions a "daily girl from the village," but she never appears and her presence is unfelt. Duncan moves from the "inviolably feminine" world of his mother's house to Priorsholt, "exclusively a house of men," and he makes this transition just as he is entering puberty, as he is assuming (or being assumed by) his sexuality.

It seemed obvious to me that both Duncan and Gerald are homosexuals, or have, as is sometimes said, "homosexual tendencies," although Gerald appears to be more successfully repressed than his nephew (sexually deviate: HOMOSEXUAL). Gerald is a wonderfully pitiful character with the inevitable disintegration of his magnificent body ("the fold in the belly, the slackening pectoral muscle"), his abject friendlessness, and subsequent loneliness, his failure as a farmer, his solitary tippling, his ineffectual decency, and, perhaps most poignantly, his inability to rehabilitate, to "make a man" out of Duncan. All of this is human, and complex, and dramatic. One feels less pity for Duncan: his stunted dumbness, both verbal and moral, prevents him from completely engaging the reader's sympathy. One wishes he inhabited himself a little less drowsily, yet while that might make him a more engaging character, it would make him a less convincing adolescent.

If the ending of *The Scapegoat* was not so unrelentingly tragic, one could almost read the book as a romantic comedy, for Duncan and Gerald do pass amusingly (and arousingly) over and around numerous hurdles and into the same bed. If their circumstances were altered—if they were not both men, not uncle and nephew, not adult and minor—the reader would, I think, be wholeheartedly rooting for them to cohabit (some readers might root anyway). After a fairly conventional courtship, involving both mistletoe and fireworks, a flooded bedroom forces the nephew and uncle to share a bed. Duncan lies in the darkness, "disquieted by the proximity of his uncle's body." Eventually he falls asleep, and while sleeping "turned over, pressing himself unconsciously against Gerald's body. . . . Gerald shifted to the edge of the bed, turned over, and tried to sleep. But sleep would not come. At last, after an hour or so, he climbed gently out of bed . . . and stole quietly downstairs." There, he drinks whiskey and "for a long time sat motionless, staring into the cooling grate." Gerald falls asleep and dreams he is hunting Duncan, a pursuit "fraught with an increasing sense of guilt and terror." He awakens from this dream "possessed by a creeping disgust, a sense of degradation which is like a physical nausea."

Guilt, terror, disgust: This is hardly the first (or last) time these emotions have been aroused. A sense of foreboding is introduced early on in the book when Gerald feels "a premonition of misfortune" immediately upon seeing Duncan's face in the arriving train carriage, and Duncan, upon encountering Gerald, feels "a disquieting sense of lurking danger." It is thereafter referred to almost constantly, and the sense of impending doom is as prevalent and intense as the sexual tension (absorbed or interested to an extreme or unreasonable degree: OBSESSED). When I first read the book I was perplexed and displeased with the overt and insistent portentousness of *The Scapegoat*—it seemed heavy handed, unnecessary, strained. I wondered why Brooke chose to develop so much of the book on this vaguely ridiculous symbolic level; it seemed a throwback to Hardy when so much of the book seemed to be looking forward. It bothered me less on my second reading because I realized how difficult, how unacceptable, it would have been for him to tell this story on the simply human level, focusing as it does on the triple bugaboos of homosexuality, incest, and pedophilia. But if the desires and actions of these risky (and potentially repellent) characters are made to seem preordained, beyond their control, Duncan and Gerald are, I think, more readily acceptable to the common mid-century reader.

In the smug revisionary way we cast our glance back over literature, I wish Brooke had been more concerned with the humans and less concerned with the gods, for the preordination seems to diminish, rather than enhance, the book's effectiveness. But the fact is that books are written when and by who they are, and as there is no changing that, there should be no wanting to change that. It seems to me that the drama and doom is unnaturally heightened in this book, but who am I to say? Drama and doom are only, after all, a matter of perspective. And for a book written where and when it was, *The Scapegoat* is almost unbelievably subversive and kinky.

As we move further and further (one hopes) from the time when homosexuality was condemned by society, books like *The Scapegoat* will become curiouser and curiouser—and queerer and queerer. In my novel *The Weekend* I have a character, who enjoys having rather pointless theoretical discussions with her friend, suggest that with the relaxation of societal constraints, the tensions that once complicated great novels no longer exist. She contends that a rigidly constraining and moralistic society that discouraged homosexuality (and divorce) offered better fodder for great fiction than a tolerant society. I hadn't read *The Scapegoat* when I wrote that scene, but it seems to be a perfect example of the kind of book that my character might have had in mind: a book that is fired in the hot, queer kiln of repression. I can think of few books that are as erotically and dramatically charged as *The Scapegoat*, or that depict so convincingly the degenerative effects of sexual repression. Gerald and Duncan are doomed by both the suppression and the expression of their urges, and that is the real tragedy of *The Scapegoat*. Repression and suppression invariably result in tension, which is good for novels, good for readers, but bad—fatal, in fact—for lives.

FRED CHAPPELL

The Most Exotic Book I Read
THE WORM OUROBOROS by E. R. Eddison

The action proper begins on the planet Mercury, though this setting bears not the least resemblance to that astronomical body. The characters are human beings like you and me, except that they are all warrior nobles of great wealth and courage and comeliness—and are accoutered with two small horns growing from their foreheads. The main action concerns a war between the nations of Demonland and Witchland and the strategies and maneuvers are described minutely and with zest.

But it is finally a bloodless war, for the antagonists bear the same relation to real personages as do the shining knights and evil mages of Edmund Spenser's romance epic, *The Faerie Queene*. The account of this conflict, and the action of the

. . . .

Fred Chappell is a poet, novelist, and essayist who lives in Greensboro, North Carolina. He has published more than twenty-five books including the poetry collections *Backsass* and *Midquest*, which was awarded the Bollingen Prize.

whole novel, is rendered in a style affectedly antique, overwrought, sometimes a little ponderous, and unsparingly gorgeous.

I suppose my comparison with Spenser will be sufficient to turn prospective readers away from E. R. Eddison's exceedingly curious novel, *The Worm Ouroboros*. Or perhaps its title will perform that feat immediately. The Ouroboros (pronounced "oo-ROB-oros") dragon is an emblem from many mythologies; in Norse legends it is called the Midgard Serpent. It is pictured as having its tail in its mouth and the circle this figure describes is a symbol of eternity, although medieval alchemists employed the symbol also to mean the hermetically secret nature of their dark art.

But Eddison claimed that his novel had no secrets, no allegorical meaning; it was only, he said, a story for its own sake. Such a statement is always suspect as a way of disarming readers, but Eddison was probably telling the truth as he knew it. He loved the purity of adventure and was something of an adventurer himself when opportunity offered. Opportunity came only annually, at vacation time from his position at the British Board of Trade. Those weeks he would take his wife and children on hiking trips through the Alps or, more frequently, into the stony fastnesses of Iceland.

For Eric Rucker Eddison (1882–1945) was a scholar, as well as a civil servant, an athlete, a traveler, and a devoted family man. He was well versed in Greek and Latin and adored classical literature. He taught himself the ancient Teutonic dialects as well as modern Icelandic and published a vigorous translation of *Egil's Saga*. This project he undertook, he said, in gratitude for the saga literature that inspired his novel, *Styrbiorn the Strong*, about the life of a rebellious Swedish prince who died in 983.

From the northern sagas, from the classical epics, from the literature of the Elizabethan Renaissance, from sources of many kinds, Eddison borrowed the trappings of his dream world and the style in which it is set forth. But *The Worm Ouroboros* is not mere pastiche. It is a strikingly original work and its debts to ancient sources only make it shine more brightly in its own right.

And shine it does, as with the hues and gleamings of jewels, for this author is infatuated with jewelry, with weapons, with gown and arras, pearled fillet and gored sleeve. He loves to overload his scenes with descriptions of furniture, precious metals, and architecture, and will go on for pages with descriptions that have the color and rich density, and for some people the indigestibility, of Christmas fruitcake.

Now that I've given fair warning, here is a smallish sample of his penchant for plenitude, one of the minor paragraphs picturing the "presence chamber" in the castle of Lord Juss of Demonland:

But a great wonder of this chamber, and a marvel to behold, was how the capital of every one of the four-and-twenty pillars was hewn from a single precious stone, carved by the hand of some sculptor of long ago into the living form of a monster: here was a harpy with screaming mouth, so wondrously cut in ochre-tinted jade it was a marvel to hear no scream from her: here in wine-yellow topaz a flying fire-drake: there a cockatrice made of a single ruby: there a star sapphire of the colour of moonlight, cut for a cyclops, so that the rays of the star trembled from his single eye: salamanders, mermaids, chimaeras, wild men o' the woods, leviathans, all hewn from faultless gems, thrice the bulk of a big man's body, velvet-dark sapphires, chrysolite, beryl, amethyst, and the yellow zircon that is like transparent gold.

I do not offer this passage as a typical sample because it is a shorter paragraph than Eddison usually prefers and much less elaborate than most in prose style. But it should give an indication that, as the sly Southern fantasist, James Branch Cabell, said, "The book, to be sure, is not for everyone." He continues: "So many persons, indeed, to whose attention I have introduced it have got from the volume only boredom that I have at last, through a series of depressing failures to communicate my enthusiasm, been reduced to concluding that a reader finds perforce in this book exceeding joy or else nothing at all,—in either case, quite unpredictable."

I do not know that I can testify to "exceeding joy" in its perusal, but I do claim abiding pleasure, a sumptuous pleasure of the kind I derive from Keats's poem *The Eve of Saint Agnes*, with its passages of swollen splendor almost decadent in their sensuousness. Do you recall the feast that Porphyry lays out for Madeline?

While he from forth the closet brought a heap
Of candied apple, quince, and plum, and gourd;
With jellies soother than the creamy curd,
And lucent syrops, tinct with cinnamon;
Manna and dates in argosy transferr'd
From Fez; and spiced dainties, every one,
From silken Samarcand to cedar'd Lebanon.

Many people peruse with lush enjoyment Keats's narrative, as well as the overblown beauties of *To Autumn*, *Ode to a Nightingale*, and *Ode on Melancholy*. Yet I think that comparatively few of them would care to read four hundred pages of prose in the same vein. If many are pleased to enter the world of the great odes, they may be almost equally pleased to escape that gloriously colored sphere. The experience of one of these poems is so intense that one might fear that prolonged exposure could only dull its savor.

Yet Keats also wrote long poems, *Endymion* and *Lamia* and *Hyperion*, in the same idiom and these poems have their partisans, too, and I count myself happily among them. I do not find this surfeit of riches an embarrassment but a thorough and languorous delight.

Perhaps someone would demur: "Ah yes, but that is Keats, and this Eddison person—surely he is not in the same league." No, I would not make that claim, and neither would my exotic novelist, for respect for the truly grand poets is one of the forces that animate his book. He imitates, he paraphrases, he is at pains to quote entire; yet he makes a completely original work.

If you read in *The Worm Ouroboros* how the Demons journeyed from Salapanta to Eshgrar Ogo; how Lord Spitfire besieged the Witches in his own castle of Owlswick; how Lord Corinius entered into Owlswick and was crowned in Spitfire's sapphire chair; how Lord Brandach Daha made a great flanking march over the mountains from Transdale; of the day of the Great Battele and the issue thereof; of how Lord Juss rode the hippogriff to Zora Rach, then you will come to the last chapter that describes the entertainment given by Lord Juss in Demonland to Queen Sophonisba. In gratitude for his opulent hospitality, the Queen takes up a little cithern, saying, "O my lord, I will sing a sonnet to thee and to you my lords and to sea-girt Demonland." And then she smites the strings and sings in a crystal voice true and delicate the song that begins "Shall I compare thee to a summer's day" and ends "So long as men can breathe, or eyes can see, / So long lives this, and this gives life to thee."

E. R. Eddison was enthralled by the jeweler's art and I have wondered if *The Worm Ouroboros* might not have been designed as an immense, highly wrought, wonderfully precious setting for this single diamond of inestimable worth, Shakespeare's Sonnet 18. Perhaps not, but for me the notion that it might have been adds to the splendor.

SVEN BIRKERTS

The Most Smokin' Book I Read
CONFESSIONS OF ZENO by Italo Svevo

I just recently reread Italo Svevo's 1923 novel *Confessions of Zeno* because I wanted to confirm for myself what I had been broadcasting for years now to students and literary friends—that this novel, ingeniously premised on the narrator's struggle to give up cigarettes, was one of the funniest ever written. Alas, the only thing I really confirmed was that memory's fabulous net had become a sieve, and that one's idea of what is and isn't comic necessarily changes a good deal over time. At moments indeed, I wondered: Had I in fact read this same work those many years ago? There was just enough sense of readerly déjà vu to persuade me I'd been in these woods before, but whatever path I'd blazed was overgrown, its many turns become strange.

....

Sven Birkerts, who lives in Arlington, Massachusetts, has published five collections of literary essays and a memoir, *My Sky Blue Trades: Growing Up Counter in a Contrary Time*. He also edits the literary journal *Agni*.

Yes, quitting smoking does figure into the *Confessions*, but only in the beginning, as a kind of launching conceit. In the counterworld of readerly retrospect, I had it situated as the central motif. Could my own years of trying to outwit nicotine have had anything to do with that predominance? Svevo's real core structuring idea—like Philip Roth's in *Portnoy's Complaint*—is that this is an analysand's report to his analyst. Could my long-term suspicion of all matters therapeutic (finally therapized out of me) have had any connection with that particular memory slip? Is this how we all give in to the lobbying of the deeper self, making the past over as an image we can live with?

As for the humor, I did, this time through, find myself utterly won over by the steady subtle irony of Svevo's presentation. Again and again I closed the book on my marking thumb, paused to let some perfectly framed observation—about marriage, fidelity, friendship—ripple its way slowly along the reading nerves. The trouble is, I'm in my late forties now and the insights that tickled me this time would surely have been lost on the thirty-year-old who preceded me. What was I so delighted by the first time around? I can't begin to guess.

Confessions of Zeno is basically the candid narration of the courtship, marriage, and business adventures of one Zeno Cosini, a merchant living in Svevo's (the author's real name was Ettore Schmitz) native Trieste in the early years of the twentieth century. Plot complications are minimal: Zeno confides how in pursuing one sister, Ada, he ended up through misunderstanding and chivalric bluster, married to another, Augusta; how he later fell into and carried on his one extramarital liaison; and how he became business partners with Ada's fool of a husband, Guido Spier.

But if the incidents do not lend themselves to dramatic paraphrase, the narration more than compensates. Zeno is one of literature's great neurotics, a worthy forerunner of Alexander Portnoy, and he unburdens himself completely in these pages. Drawn into the narrow circumference of his life and concerns, we quite forget the italicized preoccupations of the larger world. Zeno's little square of reality, like the little squares Jane Austen would crowd with the life of her day, is quite enough. This should tell you something about the author's powers of psychological observation, his ability to infuse select detail with mattering.

This infusion comes by way of voice. Svevo has created in *Confessions of Zeno* a triumph of civilized irony. I mean here irony not in its customary American sense as the inability to respond to anything seriously (e.g., the puerile public posturing of Letterman and his ilk), but irony as the accommodation experience makes to innocence, the tolerantly stoical shouldering of the disappointments of maturity. This is what I would not have been ready to appreciate at thirty; it is what so cheers me now.

If quitting smoking is incidental to Zeno's main narration, it nonetheless gives us a strong first exposure to this complex, self-conflicted man. His admission of fallibility here, in one of his very first recollections to his doctor, sets us up to heed his word on matters of larger significance:

I smoked continually, hidden in all sorts of secret places. I particularly remember one half-hour spent in a dark cellar, because I was so terribly unwell afterwards. I was with two other boys, but the only thing I remember about them is the childish clothes they wore: two pairs of short knickers which I see standing up quite solidly as if the limbs which once filled them had not yet been dissolved by time. We had a great many cigarettes and we wanted to see who could smoke most in the shortest time. I won, and stoically hid the physical distress this strange experiment caused me. Afterwards we went out into the sun-

shine again. I had to shut my eyes or I should have fainted on the spot. By degrees I recovered and boasted of my victory. Then one of the boys said; "I don't care about losing. I only smoke so long as I enjoy it."

Zeno puts himself before us in all his unreconstructed impulsiveness, but also—and this is what lifts the narration to greatness—as possessor of the bemused perspective that sees what figure such intransigent behavior cuts in the larger scheme of things. Scene after scene—I would love to cull and quote, but in fact the novel is an intimately woven fabric, its recognitions worked through in such a way that they flash forth best contextually. Could this be why the work is not better known, despite its enthusiastic boosters, James Joyce among them? (Joyce, incidentally, gave lessons in English to the young Ettore Schmitz while he lived in Trieste, and Schmitz/ Svevo's wife is widely believed to be the model for the Anna Livia Plurabelle figure in *Finnegans Wake*.) *Confessions* invites you in close, offers up secrets and admissions, but you must—through much of the novel—cup your ear against the distracting noises of the larger public world.

Have I made the book sound like something only for initiates? In a way, it is. The good news, however, is that most serious readers will eventually qualify. You need only have lived long enough to appreciate the comedy of human nature persisting in its folly against all of the contrary instructions of experience. Zeno's is a subtle and seasoned sensibility, one alert to the myriad ways in which we fail ourselves as we get older. Svevo, patron saint of the worldlywise adult, has a stereoscopic vision; one eye greets the world with naive expectation, while the other supplies the corrective understanding available only to hindsight.

"Mature" is the adjective I reach for. Another reader might reach for something a bit less benign sounding. And he would be right, too. For at the end of the novel, Svevo finally punctures the domestic frame to offer glimpses of a larger panorama. In his final pages, Zeno leaves the cozy lair of his ironies and speaks out against the world as it has become. "Our life today is poisoned to the root," he declares. "Man has ousted the beasts and trees, has poisoned the air and filled up the open spaces. Worse things may happen. That melancholy and industrious anima—man—may discover new forces and harness them to his chariot. Some such danger is in the air." What happened, of course—to Svevo and Zeno—was the First World War.

Against the backdrop of so much drolly incisive self-presentation, Zeno's modern despair stands out with an emblematic clarity. I have to shake my head. What was in my mind that I recalled the novel for so long as a comic turn on a man's inability to give up cigarettes?

PEGGY PAYNE

The Most Seductive Books I Read
LITERATURE FROM INDIA

"No one had to teach her," the novelist Anita Desai writes of a young girl's flirtatiousness in *Fasting, Feasting*. "Instinctively, she knew. The pale, pale pink sari, the slender chain of seed pearls, the fresh flowers, the demure downcast turn of the eyes, the little foot in the red slipper thrusting out suddenly like a tongue, and the laughter low and sly."

Literature about India is like this young girl: It beguiles, it seduces, it lures me. The book need not be a romance; the characters don't have to be appealing; the events can be awful; so long as the work is well written, it beckons me in a way that is sensuous and nearly irresistible, like a delicious scent drifting from an open doorway. I have followed that scent, not only to read more of these stories, but to go back to India, and to

....

Peggy Payne's novel *Sister India* was a *New York Times* Notable Book of the Year. She is author of the novel *Revelation*, and coauthor, with Allan Luks, of *The Healing Power of Doing Good*. She lives in Raleigh, North Carolina.

write my own novel *Sister India,* about a woman from eastern North Carolina living in a Hindu holy city on the Ganges.

I first visited the country for two weeks in 1978, as a twenty-nine-year-old travel writer. By the last morning of that trip, I was ready to leave, exhausted—stupefied—by the constant stimulation of unfamiliar sights and sounds and smells. Coming home, I went straight from the airport to McDonald's, craving something predictable and American.

Overwhelmed as I had been, I was only home for a few days before I wanted India back. What stayed in my mind was the memory of a particular moment in Old Delhi, an experience that embodied so much of what draws me in the books of India I love. In my first hours in the country, I'd climbed up on the high open-air bench of a rickshaw. The driver wheeled us into the flood of traffic. Then came the rush of sensations—a hot waft of sour milk from a vendor's stall, the lighted-jewel colors of saris, the noise, smoky dusk, tight-packed crowd, the flashing legs of the man pumping the pedals, rickshaws clashing together in a traffic jam, a clamor so intense and unrelenting that I couldn't notice things fast enough. Holding onto the rickshaw bench, twisting one way and another to see, I felt a falling away of wariness, as if a storm were washing clean all my windows and, with a sudden lightness of spirit, I looked out on a world that was lush, dizzying, delicious.

India's impact on my spirit had little or nothing to do with the religious aura the country is famous for. It had to do with moments on the street, when, bedazzled by the tumult, I pushed aside the usual drone of worrying and daydreaming and awoke to my senses, to what I could that moment see, hear, smell.

In the months and years—more than a decade—between that first visit and my return to India, it was books that brought back again and again that intense sensory awareness, making me want to go back and to go deeper, to write a novel set there. The stories I was reading then—by Desai, by Ruth Prawer Jhabvala, Paul Scott, Bharati Mukherjee, and Clark Blaise—did for me what that moment in Delhi had done: They freed me briefly from my own thinking, led me out of my inner world. The more recent India stories, by some of these same authors and others, continue to seduce in the same way: by telling the story, whatever it may be, through the senses. "The steam rises lazily from the surface of the tea. It is thick with the aroma of boiled milk, streaked with the perfume of cardamom and clove. It wisps and curls and rises and falls, tracing letters from some fleeting alphabet." A mere cup of tea on the third page of Manil Suri's *Death of Vishnu,* and yet it is so closely observed, so intimate that I feel first the steam against my face, and then my own surge of appetite for more such details. I read on with a heightened attentiveness to the world of the story. I want to taste the tea and feel the next paragraph's sudden gust of wind, smell the chameli flowers, and hear the faint scrape of a comb through knotted hair. No other contemporary literature so savors physical details.

Surely much of this is due to the nature of the setting and how it affects the writer's sensibility. India is so rich to the senses that to be there is to wallow in sensation; to write about India is to find ways to bring this wealth onto the page; to read the stories is to let a world of heightened sensuality unfold in the imagination. The Indian photographer Raghubir Singh noted in an essay in *Persimmon* magazine that to make a drawing with a lead pencil on white paper is a technique not native to Indian art. It was an idea that came from outside to a country that had previously made art only with color. The first impulse in getting India on paper is to let the saris bloom in emerald and tangerine; to show the shrines draped with marigold garlands, the images of deities in clashing, and often garish, pastels of cotton-candy pink and orange.

The sensory is overpowering in Indian stories because it is central to Indian culture. The physicality of Hinduism, the dominant religion, shows itself at every turn. Photographer and anthropologist Stephen Huyler explores this in *Meeting God: Elements of Hindu Devotion.* His book, which could pass for a photo-essay on color, presents the objects and practices of Hindu worship: the piled lotus blossoms and coconut offerings at a temple, the washing and anointing of images, the camphor fires and sacred waters, the shrine for daily worship in a taxicab. In Hinduism, and thus in India, physical details of life are charged with meaning. It is no surprise that the shared quality of stories about India is entrancing attention to detail.

India as a subject, as a setting, teaches a writer, much in the way that a lover teaches a lover, or a baby teaches a parent, by presenting itself, with all its particulars. As the writer pays attention, she begins, like Desai's flirtatious young girl, to know what to do.

To focus, as this careful noting of detail requires of writer and reader, has another effect that may well be part of the drawing power of the stories. To gaze upon one thing with full concentration creates a feeling of timelessness, or of abundant time (a basic principle of meditation).For a hurried and overscheduled American, that feeling can be welcome indeed. The books have other methods still of pulling me into their world. To a foreign reader, the stories remain surprising throughout, which is yet another reason to pay close attention, and thus be drawn in deeper. Tightly focused attention, with relaxation, is also the basis of deepening hypnotic experience, with the hypnotist offering spell-binding suggestions like, "let all but the sound of my voice drift away."

The riveting unpredictability of Indian stories is demonstrated in a scene in *Empire of the Soul* in which author-narrator Paul William Roberts tells of an incident in an ashram. Waking the first morning after long travel in a sweltering room he'd moved into during the night: "I rubbed my puffed eyes. It took me some moments to realize that a very small man in a fur body-suit was riffling my bag, quietly picking out items of interest and putting them to one side. 'Oi!' I yelled, leaping up. The monkey bared its teeth at me."

Reading these lines, I fully believed for several seconds that a tiny man was in the room. So much is exotic to me in these books that I soon cease to hold to my usual expectations. In immersing myself in the story, I lose the half-conscious reflex telling me to discard data that seems far fetched. The resulting sense—of a wider range of possibilities—is the cumulative effect of the many small surprises in every ordinary moment in one of these novels.

My research for my own novel was primarily the keeping of a journal of the surprises and the precise details of my experience, through all my waking hours, in my three months in Benares. I wanted to know this ancient city with its maze of narrow lanes well enough to create any scene I might later imagine taking place there. I scribbled on pocket-size notepads, each night making the day's record legible on my manual typewriter, sometimes by candlelight if the power had gone out. In this way, I took down what I saw, heard, and felt when Hindu-Muslim rioting broke out on a street, causing the city of a million people to be shut down in day-and-night curfew for weeks: I noted the troops with bamboo riot shields, the gunfire I heard one afternoon as I read in the sun on my rooftop patio. When peace came again, I jotted down the domestic details on seemingly ordinary days as I lived in an apartment with a housekeeper-cook who spoke as little English as I spoke Hindi. From my notes:

He comes in with two big sacks, goes through my room out to the balcony, doesn't say anything. I follow him. He has emptied one of the sacks, which is full of dirt, onto the balcony concrete . . . I think that this is some puja in which he is making the shape of a god in dirt. I go back to my newspaper. Then I look out . . . and there is a fire on the balcony. He has emptied the other sack—dung patties—and built a fire, to cook here . . . He brings out a pan of dough . . . I ask if I can help. He laughs . . . We both stay squatted by the fire a long time . . . It's dark . . . I can see the loaded papaya trees and stars . . . I leave him alone, try to put on my sari.

Home again in Raleigh, when I sat down at my computer to start writing *Sister India,* what I most wanted to create for a reader of my novel was the feeling of being in India, of being in the lanes, on the rooftop patios, on the riverbank bathing ghats of Benares. I had, of course, the usual fears about beginning; yet one thing I did know: that the way lay in attention to the details.

HOWARD BAHR

The Most Elegant Book I Read

LANTERNS ON THE LEVEE by William Alexander Percy

At his death in 1942, William Alexander Percy of Greenville, Mississippi, had already been outrun by time. His life spanned a period of great change in the South, from the patrician era after the Civil War to the "rise of the rednecks" during the twentieth century. He watched as machinery, paved highways, and a mobile population eroded the agrarian culture which, for Percy as for Jefferson, awoke man's better nature. Thus, when Percy composed his memoir, *Lanterns on the Levee* (1941), he set out to capture his vanishing world and "indulge a heart beginning to be fretful by repeating to it the stories it knows and loves of my own country and my own people."

In *Lanterns*, Percy speaks as planter, Southern apologist, poet, warrior, and—in a single voice—ideologue, idealist, and

....

Howard Bahr was born and reared in Mississippi. He teaches English at Motlow State Community College in Lynchburg, Tennessee. Bahr has written two highly acclaimed novels of the Civil War, *The Black Flower* and *The Year of Jubilo*.

cynic. He begins where all Southerners must: with the land. The rich alluvial plane of the Mississippi Delta is the landscape for his stories of the "children of God who took up their abode beside the waters of the great river." Percy recounts his childhood among honorable, if eccentric, relatives. He carries us to Sewanee, to the fields of France, through troubles with the Klan and the disastrous high water of 1927. Finally, he reveals in beautiful prose the soul of a man who perfectly exemplifies the title of his cousin Walker Percy's novel *The Last Gentleman*.

In his introduction to *Lanterns*, Walker Percy acknowledges reservations shared by most modern readers. His cousin's views on race—startling in his time—ring, like Faulkner's, of condescension now. So, too, does his naive defense of the sharecropping system. A friend of mine, himself a Delta native of a good family, dismisses Percy as one who spun his idle dreams in leisure gained by the sweat of others.

To the liberal mind, Will Percy remains, as his cousin wryly points out, "racist, white supremacist, reactionary, paternalist, Bourbon, etc., etc." Yet Percy was a decorated combat officer in the Great War. He stood up to the Klan, organized relief efforts in Greenville during the 1927 flood, and surrendered his freedom to raise three orphaned cousins, one of whom would become a great man of letters. When I first read *Lanterns* thirty years ago, I discovered what his distinguished cousin Walker found: "a fixed point in a confusing world." I am glad to leave Will Percy in his lofty place, for I believe he practiced noblesse oblige in as pure a distillation as men are capable of.

Percy understood his responsibility and accepted it; for him, the stairs leading earthward were well trod. His work will endure because the values at its heart—often dismissed as "genteel" and which Percy himself saw as doomed—speak to the better part of us all. The catch-all "tradition" is much abused these days, but in Percy we discover its true sense: the humility to listen to those who might have been wiser than we, perhaps a little better than we, for having accomplished the journey. "Tradition," remarked G. K. Chesterton, "refuses to submit to that arrogant oligarchy who merely happen to be walking around."

Asked to apply an adjective to *Lanterns*, I would select "elegant." I use the word in the same way Percy would, as an antonym of all that is vulgar, boorish, and stupid: a vision of the world that affirms the beautiful over the ugly, the honest over the false, and the dignity of all persons. This distinction may endow both plowman and poet with elegance, but excludes those without grace who are merely rich or powerful or smart.

The triumph of vulgarity is a prominent theme in *Lanterns*, and certainly one sadly applicable to our own millennial culture. Percy writes:

I'm unhappily convinced that our exteriors have increased in importance while our interiors have deteriorated: It is a good paint job, but the lighting and sanitation are execrable. A good world, I acknowledge, an excellent world, but poor in spirit and common as hell. Vulgarity, a contagious disease like the itch, unlike it is not a disease of the surface, but eats to the marrow.

This before discount stores, rap music, and *Beavis and Butt-Head!* To hear Percy on this theme is like reading Wordsworth's "The World Is Too Much with Us": One can only shake his head and mutter, "Man, if you thought it was bad then . . . "

But, if we admit certain things in life are constant, we can understand Percy's dismay. The enemy is the same and always seems to be winning, gnawing closer and closer not only to the marrow, but to the heart.

Small things can be illustrative. At the beginning of every semester, I am obliged to confront my students with the astonishing news that boys should remove their caps in the classroom. Sweet and decent lads, they always comply, but I can see the puzzlement in their eyes. It has never occurred to them that a hall of learning demands more decorum than the sporting-goods section at Wal-Mart. They have this from their elders, whom we can observe entering, say, New Orleans's St. Louis Cathedral wearing caps ("I'm A Coon-Ass") and T-shirts ("Jesus Is My Coach, Alabama Is My Team") and sweaty rubber shoes and fanny packs, slouching through that holy place as if it were a souvenir shop on Bourbon Street. In our culture, we no longer care to make distinctions, and we have exchanged even the pretense of Percy's "exterior" for the cheap illusion of honesty. To those who find this occasion for applause, I submit the following answer to a question on my final exam last spring:

There is also a reason for people to dislike literature. The reason literature class can be dull and difficult is because of poetry analization [sic!]. The common man dislikes poetry because he does not know the meaning of half the words being used.

Also, if one did understand the vocabulary of the author, it would still require deep thoughts from the reader to grasp the meaning of the poem.

I would probably enjoy literature, [the lad goes on,] if there was no such thing as technology. Technology has made easier for people to be lazy and simply flip on the television rather sit down and read a book.

You may supply the missing words yourself, together with the larger implications of this remarkable admission. Let us be common, then. Let us find the great voices of humanity dull and difficult. Let us, above all, celebrate laziness, avoid deep thoughts, and blame it on technology rather than our own tragic indifference. Thus the marrow goes, and all our vitals, and at last our collective soul.

My impression is that Will Percy died with that realization heavy on his heart. If so, let that be the great tragedy of his life, for he must not have known, or in his humility must not have hoped, that his voice would outlive him. "For most of us," Walker Percy says, "the communication of beauty takes two, the teacher and the hearer, the pointer and the looker." I and all his teachers have failed the student whose only response to literature was to pronounce it dull. For the moment, he is lost in the blind, gray ranks of those for whom the truly bright world must remain forever colorless, who will never know the names of birds or flowers, nor recognize a single constellation, nor understand that life is made desirable only by those things we can't understand but reach for anyhow, even in our weakness.

But must he remain lost always? Vulgarity, scuttling among us, has prevailed on every front, yet it has never, even in our deepest-shadow times, silenced the subversive voices of those like Will Percy who insist that we are better than ourselves. I like to think that the same fixed point, the same navigable star, waits for that lad as it does for us all. Maybe he will find (or, in a rare lucid moment, remember) some teacher, some pointer, and choose to lift his eyes and behold the majesty of his soul. If there were not at least a chance of that, then all teaching would be in vain, the enemy victorious, and all man's striving reduced to the meaningless noise of an Ole Miss–LSU football game.

"But there's time ahead," says Will Percy. "There is but one good life and men yearn for it and will again practice it, though of my contemporaries only the stars will see." He was right, I suppose, about the stars. But they are still there, offering hope—and who is to say that, on black winter nights in the old Delta, or in summer when fireflies rise, Will Percy does not make one among them?

PETER GAY

The Most Surprising Book I Read

I WILL BEAR WITNESS: A DIARY OF THE NAZI YEARS
by Victor Klemperer

The diaries Victor Klemperer kept during the Nazi rule of Germany produced most unexpected results when they were published there in 1995: They enjoyed astonishing sales and prompted national soul-searching. I had read about the work and the excitement, but did not consider reading the diaries until 1998 when I was asked to review the English translation of the first volume of *I Will Bear Witness*, which covered 1933–1941. I was expecting the usual—increasingly painful reminiscences of increasingly terrible days. What I got was quite unexpected: a masterpiece.

I think I know modern German literature fairly well, but I found myself unable to think of another set of diaries in German that was nearly so revealing, nearly so gripping,

....

Peter Gay is director of the New York Public Library's Center for Scholars and Writers. Gay is a recipient of the National Book Award, and his work includes a five-volume study of nineteenth-century life, *Pleasure Wars: The Bourgeois Experience: Victoria to Freud,* and the memoir *My German Question: Growing Up in Nazi Berlin*.

indeed nearly so important. The events it chronicled were not particularly new to me and yet—the book hypnotized me. Writers make pictures for readers, the better the writer, the more vivid the pictures. The pictures that Klemperer paints through his entries possessed and transmitted a palpable presence. Most unexpectedly, their clarity and sheer force reminded me of the pictures my uncle Moritz Jaschkowitz had painted for my parents and me in December 1938, upon being released from a German concentration camp after a grueling six-week imprisonment. Entranced, I quickly secured the entire diaries in German. For more than a week I was engrossed in the daily life of Victor Klemperer, his wife, Eva, and their two cats Nickelchen and Muschel—the last two by no means insignificant actors in this domestic drama. When Nickelchen dies, the Klemperers mourn as though they had lost a close and beloved relative.

What made the diaries especially unexpected was the character of its source. Klemperer had been appointed professor of Romance languages and literature at the Dresden Technical University—one of Germany's lesser centers of higher learning—in 1920, at age thirty-nine. Not that he failed to work diligently at his trade: Concentrating on the seventeenth and eighteenth centuries, he published histories of French literature from the Renaissance to recent times, and specialized monographs. But he remained mired in a minor faculty of a minor university in part because he was a liberal Voltairian, a style of thinking that fitted ill into the German perception of the "shallow" French Enlightenment; in part because he seemed to his "betters," with his excursions into cultural history, not fixated enough on pure literature; in part, too, because he wrote too well in defiance of the dominant German academic style. As a young man, he had done literary journalism, and clarity was, at least for many of his fellow scholars, not a virtue but a vice. At the same time, courageous as he was in swimming against the German academic stream, there was something less than first-rate about his mind. We may appreciate his liberalism, his Francophilia, but there is nothing particularly memorable about his work. That this minor writer should have produced so extraordinary a document makes him, and his masterpiece, truly unexpected.

It seems virtually certain that Klemperer would have found his sudden fame surprising. But it is equally clear that the diary mattered to him; he kept adding to it, even though its discovery by authorities would have meant his death. And in May 1942, he noted, in a phrase that has become famous: "I continue to write. This is my heroics. I want to bear witness, precise witness, until the very end."

Still, this proud program is a far cry from the stature his accidental book has acquired, decades after his death in 1960. Historians of the Nazi period generally agree that the Klemperer diary is an indispensable source for any serious study of Hitler's Thousand Year Reich. It provides a full account of the sadistic way the Nazi regime tightened the noose around Jews living in Germany: the government-sponsored national pogrom known as the Kristallnacht, the exclusion of Jews from the professions, the pitiless despoiling of Jews of their fortunes and their property, and (near the end of the period this volume covers) the decree that Jews must wear a yellow star, and wear it prominently.

He writes:

August 17, 1937: "In [Der] Stürmer (which is displayed at every corner) I recently saw a picture: two girls in swimming costumes at a seaside resort. Above it: 'Prohibited for Jews,' underneath it: 'How nice that it's just for us now.' "

November 28, 1937: "The day before yesterday a speech by Goebbels: We have weeded out the Jews, and the layout of our newspapers is better than ever before! Mocks himself without knowing it."

His work achieves a cumulative power, in part, because his memories are recorded in real time, and are unretouched. The sequence of the dehumanization of Jews stands before the reader, each new piece of chicanery or brutality captured at the moment of its perpetration. The spontaneity of the entries has been preserved, so that shifts in Klemperer's opinions, inconsistencies, even certain absurdities remain to make this a document that virtually breathes.

He writes:

March 30, 1938: "*Sometimes I draw a certain comfort precisely from the terrible hopelessness of the situation. This is a peak; nothing, neither good nor evil, can remain in a state of superlatives. The hubris, the brutality, the cynicism, of the victors in their 'election speeches' is so monstrous, the threats and abuses of other countries assumes such lunatic forms, that the counter-stroke must come some time.*"

July 27, 1938: "*Rock-bottom days. It is absurd to go on hoping for change. They are so firmly in the saddle, in Germany people are content, abroad they're keeping their heads down.*"

Though Klemperer's work reflects the day to day, it is not without literary excitement. Such moments are rare, but when they occur, they are particularly powerful because they are unexpected. In June 1941, Klemperer was sentenced to prison and remained there for nine days, for failing to black out one of his windows at night earlier that year. In general, both Klemperers were very conscientious about this order to keep enemy aircraft from seeing any lights on the ground. But just once they had kept one of their windows uncovered in a lit room. The policeman who came to their place was cordial enough—"one of the honest and friendly people from our station who carried out the supervision of the Jews very courteously"—but since the Klemperers had been denounced by a neighbor, it was impossible for him to overlook this breach of regulations. Several months later, Klemperer went to the jail providently equipped with writing materials and several books. But all this was taken away from him, including his glasses, and he spent several days in solitary confinement, with nothing to occupy him but his thoughts. Finally released on July 1, he sat down and recorded his experience, bit by bit. The episode occupies twenty-five closely printed pages, titled "CELL 89, 23rd JUNE–1st JULY 1941," and with his precision, his uncanny gift for recall, his need to get it all down and get it right, this set piece approaches the power of Dostoyevsky— even surpasses it, for what he had recaptured was what he called "one of the most agonizing times of my life." It was sheer reality.

Yet this document of increasing horror is not without its humor—another surprising feature—involuntary humor to be sure. Late in 1935, to save money on taxis to travel between Dresden and his family's little, recently built, country house, Klemperer takes driving lessons. At first, he would come home "completely shattered and soaked through," but he slowly learns to enjoy driving a car, and he takes great pride in his very limited, very awkward progress. But he has endless troubles starting the car, he gets caught in a couple of minor accidents that make him sweat, he runs out of gas, he drives no faster than thirty miles per hour. Worst of all, he continually dents the mudguard, as he hits the relatively narrow garden gate and the garden wall on his way into or out of his property. All these excruciating details find their way into the diary as moments of rather pitiful comedy. Only gradually, he becomes more proficient as a driver. But this twisted road to competence is, of course, about as much humor as the diary contains.

If we take the second volume of Klemperer's diary, *I Will Bear Witness: A Diary of the Nazi Years, 1942–1945,* into account, the most unexpected event of all is Klemperer's survival. Born into a Jewish family—his father was a rabbi—he had early converted to Protestantism, a change of self-presentation that the Nazis, we know, wholly disregarded. To the Nazis, he was a Jew. Yet there was no move to deport him to a death camp in the east because his wife, Eva, was an "Aryan." By the peculiar logic of Nazi ideology, such a Jew was "safe" enough, if impoverished, despised, and isolated, as long as his Gentile wife did not divorce him, or die. At least as late as early 1945, this shield held firm. But then, the Nazis changed their policy abruptly. However, in February 1945, as Klemperer was about to be deported, the Allies literally saved his life through their bombing of Dresden. After being separated briefly in the general confusion, Victor and Eva Klemperer found one another, and Eva's first act was to snip off her husband's yellow star. Thus Victor Klemperer owed his survival to a crazy Nazi decree and a harsh act of war. What could be more surprising than this?

MARVIN HUNT

The Most Disappointing Book I Read
HOTEL HONOLULU by Paul Theroux

Disappointment, like illness, comes in acute and chronic forms. You back the wrong horse and you're suddenly bereft, cut to the quick. Attendant upon the moment is a diffused anger at all the inscrutable factors—fate, bad luck, family curses—that led you to put good money on a horse that should have been named Future Glue. Intense but ephemeral, this kind of disappointment fades quickly. A few miles down the road from the track you're looking forward to drinks and dinner. Unless, that is, with this wager you've lost the house, blown the family apart. In this case you experience something deeper and graver than acute disappointment, something fraught with really troubling consequences for a life rather than an afternoon.

. . . .

Marvin Hunt's travel stories have been widely published in magazines and newspapers, including the *New York Times* and the *Washington Post*. A specialist in the English Renaissance, he teaches English at North Carolina State University.

Because the relationship between readers and writers is so intimate, readers are susceptible to especially painful disappointments, of both acute and chronic versions. I've read armloads of books (most lavishly financed and heavily promoted) that acutely disappointed me, some by writers who had engaged me deeply. William Least-Heat Moon comes to mind. I loved and earnestly championed his *Blue Highways,* an account of traveling America's back roads, so when he bombed with *River-Horse,* I vented my disappointment in an angry review, then forgot about it. No scars, no lingering concerns.

But passionate and committed readers open themselves to a deeper, impossible-to-slake disappointment when, for all the right reasons, they back writers who, after many years and books, betray their devotion. It's like pulling back the curtain and discovering the Wizard of Oz, a small man with weird hair speaking in a strange voice through an amplifier.

Such is my experience with Paul Theroux, author of several shelves of novels, travel books, story and essay collections, even a book of literary criticism. Theroux's most recent novel, *Hotel Honolulu*—the most disappointing book I've ever read—has just been published.

Deep disappointments have histories. In 1978, my friend Tom Eamon and I were exchanging favorites in a sort of two-person book club. We'd spent the summer reading books set in the Indian subcontinent—V. S. Naipaul's *An Area of Darkness,* Peter Matthiessen's *The Snow Leopard*, Louise Hillary's *High Time* and *A Yak for Christmas*. One day Tom brought over a book whose dust cover was a lurid montage of trains and people shot in exotic places. It was *The Great Railway Bazaar* by Paul Theroux.

The Great Railway Bazaar turned out to be much more than a good read. Theroux's journey through Europe and Asia by train instantly identified travel writing for me in a way I had never before recognized, bringing into focus a vast library stretching back to Homer that included every inveterate roamer of the planet who wrote about what he encountered. Terribly envious and even covetous of *The Great Railway Bazaar,* I knew then that I wanted to write about travel.

Over the next year I read everything Theroux had published, relishing his African novels *Fong and the Indians* and *Jungle Lovers* and *Saint Jack*, which was set in Singapore. Theroux's expatriate sensibility, his exotic settings, quirky characters, and elegant prose style, defined my unspoken aspirations. I ordered first editions of his books. I wrote him admiring letters to which he replied in short, friendly cards, written in a hand that flowed so freely as to be unreadable in places. Each one I tucked away into one of his books that now made up a substantial part of my young library. I was an apostle during those years. Anytime the conversation turned to books, I would ask, "Have you read Paul Theroux?"

I wasn't alone in my devotion. For much of the next decade Theroux was the darling of critics, who compared him to Kipling and Graham Greene. At this time I became a doctoral student in English, and I remember feeling a special confidence about my acumen that had something to do with my sense that, backing Paul Theroux, I had backed the right horse. I had a good nose for this sort of thing. This confidence made for better work, I think, no matter whether I was writing about John Webster (whose plays Theroux taught in Singapore) or John Keats or T. S. Eliot. My professors warmly endorsed them, meaning that I made good grades. In 1983, when *The Mosquito Coast* garnered high praise from every corner and confirmed Theroux as a major American writer, I crowed loudly. My horse had won. I wrote Theroux saying that if he kept up this level of writing he could as well count on a Nobel Prize.

Then came *O-Zone,* the first of Theroux's miscreated books. Fat and fatuous and lamely imagined, this futuristic thriller remains the only one of Theroux's books I couldn't finish. A sudden, unexpected, acute disappointment, I admit. I was stunned but saw no reason to reassess this very special writer, even when that resolve was tested by the awful *Chicago Loop,* which Theroux ought to have aborted.

These were dark times for Theroux's work. Critics had begun to sour on this too-prolific writer. They attacked his travel writing as misanthropic and judged his novels weird or clumsy or uninteresting. Like a landslide, a mindless, irresistible predisposition arose among them to write Theroux off as a failure, sometimes, it seemed, without even reading what he wrote. I was outraged. When *The Happy Isles of Oceania* was dismissed as an aloof, sneering, meanspirited tour of the equatorial Pacific, I wrote an angry letter to the *New York Times Book Review* insisting that if readers wanted brochures they should visit travel agencies. But if they wanted real books about real people they should read Theroux. I received a warm thank-you note from the author—and another from his editor.

But the joke was on me. With *My Secret History* Theroux began to write about himself under the thinnest veil of fiction. This move took his writing in a disastrous new direction, seeming, in hindsight, to signal a failure of the imagination. No longer were characters real inventions; now they were transparent guises of people and events in his own life, snatched from Africa, Singapore, London, and Cape Cod. And, of course, Theroux was the hero of this ongoing roman à clef, which continued with *My Other Life,* in which he wrote disparagingly about friends such as Naipaul, and even his wife, whom he had recently divorced. It was a gratuitous, exploitative, and cruel book that prompted a scathing rebuke from his brother, Alexander, who himself aired some very dirty family laundry.

My Other Life was a betrayal not only of family and friends, but

also of his best, most attentive readers. Then came a gratuitous profile of recently deceased Bruce Chatwin in Granta that reeked of
envy. This was a turning point for me. Egoism had always been a
latent characteristic of Theroux's work, but prior to achieving fame
and fortune, he'd suppressed that tendency in favor of imagining a
world outside himself. Now, he was becoming more self-involved,
unable to see anything but himself. More and more he wrote, it
seemed, primarily to justify his own problematic history. By the new
millennium Paul Theroux no longer resembled the writer on whom I
had staked so much in the 1970s and 1980s.

So I could only hope that with *Hotel Honolulu,* this wunderkind
of 1970s American writers would reverse his slide into self-aggran-
dizing mediocrity. Alas, no. This novel, another thinly veiled book
about himself, quickly devolves into an homage to its creator. The
parallels are blatant. A decade ago Theroux, having divorced his
wife, moved to Hawaii, where he remarried. From this island bas-
tion Theroux has battled critical opprobrium and popular decline.
He took up beekeeping.

The unnamed narrator of *Hotel Honolulu* is a novelist who has
abandoned his turned-south writing career, moved to Hawaii and
landed a job managing a seen-better-days hotel near the beach in
Honolulu. A rank howlie, he marries a local girl, Sweetie, the illegiti-
mate daughter of JFK, and is now the father of the impossibly precocious five year-old named—what else?—Rose. His work tending to
vacationers' needs is tawdry, voyeuristic, and humiliating. The kinky
sexual episodes he witnesses, the murders and suicides he recounts
(sometimes in detail unavailable to a first-person narrator), the
degradations and embarrassments readers must endure, take place
in a physical environment—perhaps Nature's closest approximation
of Paradise—that never comes to life. The "novel" ends with the narrator becoming a beekeeper.

Appropriating real people—the late Leon Edel, renowned biographer of Henry James, appears as the narrator's admirer—this book is not so much a novel as a series of exploitative vignettes. Except for some crisply written sections, it disappoints on virtually every level. In fact, the true measure of *Hotel Honolulu* might not be the narrator—or even the character of Lionberg, Theroux's alter ego—but the hotel itself, a decaying relic several streets back of the beach that collapses upon the reader like a large, frail marriage.

Okay, maybe that's too much. Having a writer go south on you isn't in the same league with losing the house and family, at the track or elsewhere. But we shouldn't mistake the depth of the loss, which is like the death of an old friendship, the kind of experience Theroux chronicles in *Sir Vidia's Shadow*, the history of his thirty-year relationship with V. S. Naipual. There are material consequences, too, of course. Anyone interested in a set of first editions I paid top dollar for? On a deeper level, Theroux's descent calls my taste and acumen into question, just as surely as his ascent once confirmed them—only now I'm older, and the past is irretrievable.

Here's the real problem for me: The big risk of investing yourself in a living writer, as opposed to a dead one, is that the outcome is still unknown. Life is process, and backing it is always a gamble. And hope springs eternal. Perhaps Theroux will turn out to be a version of Hemingway, a writer with a reserve of genius not yet realized, who will rise from the rubble of *Hotel Honolulu* like a Phoenix. Maybe, like Hemingway slouching toward *A Moveable Feast*, his time will come around again, he'll resurrect himself and win the Nobel Prize. I have his reply to my suggestion tucked away in one of his books. First editions all, I don't think I'll unload them at a loss just yet. I may be cheap but I'm not free.

DORIS BETTS

The Most Unpleasant Book I Read
AMERICAN PSYCHO by Bret Easton Ellis

I am a reader addict. If I don't have a book to read, I need a magazine or newspaper. If I can't find those, cereal boxes, toothpaste tubes, and prescription pill bottles will do.

Like all true reader-addicts, I have had to resign myself to two inescapable truths: Life produces so many interruptions that I can't spend all my time reading; and life is also so short I can't read everything that I want to, which is everything. So I feel both famished and discouraged whenever I gawk at a library's vast, packed shelves.

Other book-devourers who reach this stage decide to specialize. Some try to read every mystery; others choose only books about food, or cats, or war. But some, like me, continue

. . . .

Doris Betts is Alumni Distinguished Professor of English at the University of North Carolina at Chapel Hill. She has written nine books of fiction, including the novel *Souls Raised from the Dead,* which won the Southern Book Critics Circle Award in 1994, and the story collection *Beasts of the Southern Wild and Other Stories,* which was a finalist for the National Book Award in 1973.

to plunder every category in the Dewey Decimal System, now only tasting more volumes than we swallow whole. The books I wish I hadn't read could fill a book. And if such a book were ever compiled, here's exactly how it would begin: with Bret Easton Ellis's novel *American Psycho*, the most unpleasant book I read.

The strange thing is, I knew in advance what I was in for. One female staff reader at Simon & Schuster, which had paid Ellis a fat advance for the work, stopped reading in midmanuscript, refusing to read another page even if it meant her job. The onslaught of salacious details of violence, especially brutality against women, were more than she or her employer could take—ultimately, Simon & Schuster refused to publish the novel.

Vintage Books finally issued *American Psycho* in 1991. *Publishers Weekly* called it "a grisly, gritty gross-out." "Snuff This Book" read the headline over the major pan delivered in the *New York Times Book Review*. The novel quickly made the Catholic black list. Norman Mailer praised it.

Then and since, most of its readers have expressed disgust, and many have wondered whether freedom of speech should allow such explicit, detailed sadism.

So why did I read it? As a teacher at the University of North Carolina at Chapel Hill, I usually can't appreciate the music college students like, but I've tried to read those books they circulate outside the syllabus. A decade ago when Ellis's novel appeared, it became part of a buzz in New York publishing circles about the "Brat Pack" writers, and my present need of examples illustrates how brief such buzzes are. The Brat Pack included Jay McInerney (*Bright Lights, Big City*), Tama Janowitz (*Slaves of New York*), and Ellis himself. These youthful writers attracted a niche audience of campus readers. Ellis, only twenty, was a student at Bennington when his first novel (*Less*

Than Zero) appeared, with its theme of "casual nihilism." So, grimly, I assigned myself his second book.

Briefly, *American Psycho* explores the daytime routines and nighttime cruel acts of rich Manhattanite Patrick Bateman, a worst case of a 1980's successful Yuppie.

Its rambling plot enumerates more fashion details and brand names than readers care to know. Bateman's daytime life is mind numbing in its false sophistication. He and other rich-but-shallow Yuppies discuss trends and fads with the urgency bishops once gave to rating heresies; so the book's first third depicts in excruciating detail which bottled waters are preferable, which behaviors au courant.

Below the surface of this Yuppie dream of financial success and boring conformity, Bateman's inner hollow life is far more meaningless than that of Dr. Jekyll; to relieve his boredom—which also bores the reader—his Mr. Hyde self begins deliberately kicking the stumps of beggar amputees, disemboweling dogs, stabbing a homeless man, etc. Finally he murders gays and prostitutes, moves on to invent horrendous sexual tortures, decapitates and dismembers victims, indulges in cannibalism and so on.

"And so on" means that so long a sequence of horrors almost turns into another boring list, that the reader's state of constant shock can hardly be sustained. While Bateman moonlights as a modern Jack the Ripper, the reader goes numb, as only so many words are available to render repeated dreadful acts. Critic Naomi Wolf became desensitized not only by Bateman's superficial big-city life, but also by his long-winded, violent pornography, which gradually wore out its power. In Bateman's world, the horrors became mundane and frequent.

The best works of true crime or horror use violence and mayhem to raise questions about human potential. Was Ellis's point to make me callous, even to the unspeakable? Or was Ellis implying that a greedy and self-centered lifestyle produces monsters who can only alleviate emptiness by porn and gore—preferably well mixed?

After one reviewer got my hackles up by comparing Ellis to Dostoyevsky, I went back to read *Less Than Zero*, that first Brat Pack novel (1986) from his student days. There his collegiate narrator, somewhat resembling Dustin Hoffman in *The Graduate,* comes home for Christmas in Los Angeles. Clay is a passive spectator to circles of a contemporary evil inferno but, unlike Dante, is no judge but a voyeur who cannot tear his wide, fascinated eyes away. He keeps passively watching a paid gay sex act, seems to acquiesce when a twelve-year-old girl is tied to a bedpost for gang rape, joins other youths on drugs enjoying films that combine sex with torture. If Bateman was a prototypical *American Psycho,* Clay in this first novel is his kid brother, numb to moral values, apathetic when they are breached. "Not there," he says of himself.

How shall we readers distinguish between those authors who understand evil and depict it unflinchingly, and those who seem almost to enjoy degradation? Feminist critics have detected genuine sick pleasure in the way *American Psycho* relishes the mutilation of women's bodies.

Some readers might say that *American Psycho* has inflamed such vehement criticism because it challenges societal norms. In their day, works by Henry Miller, D. H. Lawrence, and many other now-acclaimed writers were denounced as obscene. But there is an important difference: those earlier writers defied tradition, propriety, and restraint in order to express a call to sensuality, to Eros, to celebrate life. The movement of their work is expansive; it angles toward embrace.

American Psycho moves in the opposite direction, away from regard for life, for humanity, even the self. The body is not for pro-creation, not for pleasure, but for pain.

Roger Shattuck examines this distinction in his book *Forbidden Knowledge,* describing how today's exploration of raw experience as an end in itself differs from the use of experience as a means to wisdom. A National Book Award–winning philosopher and critic, Shattuck argues that some books might actually be toxic and concludes that "the time has come to think as intently about limits as about liberation." How could such limits be set? Who would set them? How could they be enforced?

And, is *American Psycho* more toxic than news reports, for example, about Jeffrey Dahmer, more pointless than the school shootings at Columbine? Did Norman Bates inspire this novel as he did the film *Psycho,* with its memorable attack on Janet Leigh in the shower?

These killers are part of contemporary reality. John Wayne Gacy and the Moor Murderers actually performed hideous acts of torture on the young, while *American Psycho* is a work of fiction. In fact, by the novel's end most readers will accept that verdict, will realize that the character Bateman is mad, that we have been immersed not in experiencing his terrible crimes, but only in the sick fantasies of his mind. The novel itself is 399 pages of the fantasies in Ellis's mind. And, while reading, we have made those fantasies a part of our own minds. Shattuck thinks that "normal" people read such books out of curiosity.

Yes, I'd been curious. Was that why my students—mostly bright and caring people—stained their own minds with the detritus from that of Brett Easton Ellis?

Admirers of the novel compare it to other "transgressive" works by writers such as William Burroughs, the Marquis de Sade, Celine, and John Rechy, who document the darkest sides of both fantasy and experience. Such commentators cite the reality of a human "shadow self " identified in Jungian psychology, that self-centered Id that relishes meanness for its own sake and becomes explosive if unacknowledged and uncontrolled. This view is paralleled in many of the world's religions and mythologies, where Original Sin, an Evil Twin, the powers of Chaos must all be admitted, confronted, and understood.

Do such books fulfill that secret human need? Or should such books be banned as some prefer, saying that if DDT pollutes the physical world, we can also pollute the mental and spiritual world? While agreeing that "no maiden was ever seduced by a book," they point out that many real-life murderers and torturers have had closets full of "transgressive" books and snuff films, that the Moor Murderers tape-recorded the screams of tortured children so they could continue to enjoy them after the victims were dead.

All that horror is true, but I must stand with those who believe new evils are wrought by censorship, and that few real tortures have been any worse than those performed by respectable people against heresy and blasphemy.

So long as there is freedom to write such books, to publish and sell them, there will be readers who—from curiosity or secret release or to feed their worst selves—read one, many, or all. Most of us don't persist, as there are opposite freedoms, like that of Simon & Schuster to choose not to publish this one, and the public's choice of what to buy and read.

Bret Easton Ellis has published three later works of fiction besides the two I've mentioned. I have not read them, and I do not plan to do so.

LEE SMITH

The Most Luminous Book I Read

THE LITTLE LOCKSMITH by Katharine Butler Hathaway

Castine, Maine—I wake early here, in our corner bedroom already flooded with light. Beyond the window, light winks on the shining water of Wadsworth Cove and glows in the mist that still shrouds Islesboro and Belfast and the Camden hills beyond; light rolls golden up the hayfield on the point. I'm instantly wide awake, so wide awake it's scary. I get up immediately, pull on some jeans and sneakers, go downstairs, feed the dog, and together we walk down the path through the tall grass and out to the gravelly half-moon beach.

The birch trees rustle in their papery, conspiratorial way. Birds cry out. Little white waves break on the shore. But this water is cold, not like the Myrtle Beach or Wrightsville Beach of my youth, where you could jump the waves all day and they would pick you up and hold you in their warm, salty embrace.

. . . .

Lee Smith is the author of fourteen books, including the novels *Fair and Tender Ladies, Oral History,* and *The Last Girls*, and the short story collections *Cakewalk* and *News of the Spirit*.

No, this water would kill you; you have to enter and exit quickly, shivering. There's no boardwalk, no dance pavilion, no Krispy Kreme doughnut place. It's beautiful here, but it's a severe, rigorous beauty. A loon calls across the water. Light leaps off the little waves like a thousand arrows aimed at me; I fish my sunglasses out of my pocket and put them on, though it isn't even seven A.M. I breathe deeply in this chilly air, which seems strangely effervescent, like champagne.

And actually I'm feeling a little intoxicated, the way I often feel here, the way I always feel when I'm starting a new novel, which I am—or will, as soon as I get up my nerve. It's that old disorientation, that scary lightness of being, that moment before you spring off the diving board straight out into the shining air, headfirst. You could kill yourself, and you know it, and you've got to get to the point where you don't care.

I'm not quite there yet.

But by fortunate chance, I'm here in Castine, a place I associate with taking risks and writing. I've got three weeks in a rented house with an old dog and an accommodating husband who doesn't care how crazy I act when I'm starting a novel. I gulp down two Advils because I have a long hill to climb and I've got plantar's fasciitis now, which is a kind of arthritis you get in your feet when you're old, which I am. This is a true thing I have only recently discovered; it is like an ugly scab I never noticed before but now I can't quit picking at.

In my windbreaker's side pocket I've got my talisman, my Bible, my lucky charm: my current copy of *The Little Locksmith,* by Katharine Butler Hathaway. I've given away at least a dozen copies of this memoir since it was republished by the Feminist Press, after Maine writer Alix Kates Schulman found it in a second-hand bookstore and brought it to their attention. It first came to me here, two years ago, when I really needed it—as books so often do.

I give it mostly to my sister writers (because it is one of the best books ever written about writing) but also to anyone facing challenges of any sort, for it is truly a story of transformation, one of the finest spiritual autobiographies ever written. Basically I give it to people I love, trusting that it will mean as much to them as it has to me. As Katharine herself says (and I'm going to call her Katharine in this essay because I consider her my true friend), hers was "a lonely voyage of discovery" that began when she decided that she "couldn't let fear decide things" for her, when she decided "to follow the single, fresh living voice" of her "own destiny."

Indeed this is a fearless book, as well as an entirely original one. It is not at all like anything else I have ever read. Though she was very frail, Katharine was tough. She was also precise. Her book is like an exquisitely cut jewel—a topaz, I think, rather than a diamond (maybe I think this because it's my own birthstone, but everybody who reads this books wants to claim it as her own). Each facet reveals a new insight or an indelible image. Hold it up to the window, turn it this way and that, and it will cast off rays of light in every direction, piercing even the oddest, most secret depths of the reader's psyche. *The Little Locksmith* tells the story of how Katharine overcame her severe physical and psychological handicaps (her "predicament," she calls it) and came to this tiny, out-of-the-way village on Maine's stern rocky coast where, against her family's wishes and all advice, she bought a house on Court Street, overlooking the harbor.

I'm headed up there now. I give Gracie a biscuit and turn left off the lane to walk through the luminous ground mist along the old British Canal, then right on Route 166 up the steep road into town. Katharine's book fits easily in the pocket of my windbreaker; it's small, like its author.

Born in 1890 into a loving, prosperous family in Salem,

Massachusetts, Katharine Butler Hathaway was stricken by spinal tuberculosis at age five and "changed from a rushing, laughing child into a bedridden, meditative one." The most advanced medical theories of the day dictated her new "horizontal life," which would last for ten years:

For the doctor's treatment consisted in my being strapped down very tight on a stretcher, on a very hard sloping bed, with my shoulders pressed against a hard pad. My head was kept from sinking down on my chest by means of a leather halter attached to a rope which went through a pulley at the head of the bed. On the end of the rope hung a five-pound iron weight. This mechanism held me a prisoner for twenty-four hours a day, without the freedom to turn or twist my body or let my chin move out of its up-tilted position in the leather halter, except to go from side to side. My back was supposed to be kept absolutely still.

However, Katharine's "hands and arms and mind were free. . . . I held my pencil and pad of paper up in the air above my face, and I wrote microscopic letters and poems, and made little books of stories, and very tiny pictures" along with paper dolls, dollhouse furniture, and doll clothes. In these Brontë-like pursuits she was accompanied always by her loving brothers and sister, who "took it for granted that no other amusement was really interesting compared with drawing or writing or making something" and made her bedroom "the natural center of the house for the others."

Yet her natural "happy, sparkling" sense of herself was challenged by the "ghoulish pleasure" of visiting children who stared at her halter and strap, and by their parents' overt pity. Worst of all was the occasional appearance of the hunchback who came to the house to fix locks. Katharine had been told that without the treatment she would have grown up to be like him. Yet she felt the "truth was that I really belonged with him, even if it was never going to show. I was secretly linked with him, and I felt a strong, childish, amorous pity and desire toward him, so that there was even a queer erotic charm for me about his gray shabby clothes, the strange awful peak in his back, and his cross, unapproachable sadness which made him not look at other people, not even me lying on my bed and staring sideways at him."

When Katharine was finally released from her board at fifteen, this suspicion was confirmed: "That person in the mirror couldn't be me! I felt inside like a healthy, ordinary lucky person. . . . A hideous disguise had been cast over me." Katharine's refusal to accept her limitations—including her desire for sexual love, which shocked many readers when this book was first published in 1943—strikes me as an act of great courage. She always "believed passionately that every human being could be happy," including herself.

She was admitted to Radcliffe College, where she spent three blissful years as a special student and made several good friends for life: smart, artistic, bohemian girls among whom she flourished in her "perfect imitation of a grown-up person, one who was noted for a sort of peaceful wise detachment," whose "curious, impersonal life gave her an enviable agelessness and liberty." But this self fell apart when she returned home after college. She sank into a deep depression and "toxic fear" (agoraphobia), a complete disintegration from which she finally emerged through her old childhood pastime, writing.

"A block of paper and a pencil had saved me. They had not only saved me by satisfying my hunger and canceling the overwhelming terror of the universe, but they gave me also an inexhaustible form of entertainment because they gave me, or seemed to give me, the equivalent of all sorts of human experience. There was no end and no limit to this kind of living." Her writing restored "the greatest visible world" to her as "an object of love, full of mystery and meaning." Thus she "got hold of a most extraordinary joy."

When I first read these words, I was at a pretty low ebb myself, worried about a lot of things, in despair about a few of them. For one thing, I was having a hard time with a book I'd been working on for a long time. Katharine's comments about writing itself seemed like a beam of light falling upon me. Thinking of myself as a professional writer for so long—even, God forbid, as a teacher of writing—I had clean forgotten the other great function of this activity: writing as solace, as a way toward self-understanding, as self-repair. You don't have to publish everything, I realized. Just write it for yourself. I picked up my pen and wrote my way through a couple of my own "predicaments."

Katharine's transformation was further accomplished by buying the house I'm standing in front of right now, atop this windy hill. When an unexpected legacy allowed her to conceive her grand plan of living independently, she first thought she'd buy "a thimble . . . something mignonne and doll-like," just like herself: "a very small childish spinster . . . a little oddity, deformed and ashamed and shy." Instead, she found herself "awestruck by the force of destiny" when she came upon this "very large high square house on Penobscot Bay overlooking the Bagaduce River and the islands and the Cape Rozier Hills. . . . I knew that whether I liked it or not this at last was my house."

Somebody else lives in Katharine's house now, of course, and yet it's all here, just as she described it: the bright sun, the endless wind, the flower-studded fields dropping down to the harbor. It's easy to imagine her sitting on this wide stone doorsill, "rapturously at home," as she often sat that first summer while workmen hammered and painted and restored the chimneys, the twelve-paned windows, the "old heavy original door" whose "panels, set with narrow, handmade moldings, made a great serene sign of the cross—two short panels at the top and two tall ones below." Indeed it is still the "sober, grand, romantic house" which was to be her "rebellion against cuteness. . . . I wanted room to find out what I really was, and room to be whatever I really was." *The Little Locksmith* is the story of how Katharine grew to fit her house, shedding her self-identity of cripple and assuming her true identity as artist.

Katharine's transformation, her "new world" is described in terms of light: "I had never seen a world so gilded and so richly bathed and blessed by such a benign sun as that world was by that sun. The sun seemed to pour down a lavish, golden, invulnerable contentment on everything, on people, houses, animals, fields—and a sweetness like the sweetness of passion." Which would come to her, too, against all odds, in "that graceful sitting room, full of sunshine, on the southwest corner, the room destined to become the one most used and most loved of the entire house. Wonderful, strange things happened to me and were said to me there, which I never could have believed were possible at the time when I was so eagerly preparing it."

Eventually, Katharine left this house and found her way to Paris, where she became part of a vibrant circle of writers and artists. "Everything is different since Castine. Yet it all began there. For there and then I first began in utter ignorance and naïveté and to heed the little voice which spoke to me and told me which way to turn." Eventually Katharine came to believe that this was in fact the voice of God; she wrote that *The Little Locksmith* was "going to be my bread-and-butter letter to God, for a lovely visit on the earth." Her happiness was complete when she fell in love with Dan Hathaway of Marblehead, Mass., marrying him in 1932. Though the Depression forced them to sell Katharine's beloved house, perhaps it had already served its purpose; the couple ended up blissfully happy in a cozier house in Blue Hill, Maine—just up the peninsula from Castine.

Chapters of *The Little Locksmith* were being serially published in the *Atlantic Monthly* magazine in the fall of 1942—to great acclaim and national interest—when Katharine's precarious health "went haywire." "At present," she wrote from the Blue Hill Hospital in early December, "my only comfortable posture is on the knees with head bent down in front of me, like a snail or an unborn child. Only then can I breathe." She died on Christmas Eve; *The Little Locksmith* was published posthumously the following year. Writing it meant everything to her ("I love this book and I can hardly bear to leave it now" she wrote at the end); its publication seemed almost irrelevant.

And yet it's still here. This book is in my pocket. This house is still here on its hill, everything just as Katharine described it: the fanlight over the heavy door; the twelve-paneled windows; the brick path, lovingly uncovered; the swaying willows; and most of all, the light. The entire "great visible world" is here before us, our own real world, where amazing things are possible. It's all still here for us all, if we can overcome our fears and summon the courage to trust ourselves, to listen to whatever voice speaks within us, to trust Katharine's "magic of transformation." I check my watch: 7:45. There's still time to walk back down the hill, make some coffee for my husband, if he hasn't done it already, and maybe—who knows?—start a novel.

ACKNOWLEDGMENTS

These essays originally appeared in the *News & Observer* of Raleigh, North Carolina. Special thanks are due to my editors at the newspaper, especially Melanie Sill, Anders Gyllenhaal, Felicia Gressette, and Suzanne Brown, who provided invaluable support and guidance throughout the two-year project. Copyeditors Nell D. Joslin, Debra H. Boyette, Pamela B. Nelson, and Marcy Smith Rice guarded against lapses in clarity and grammar. Page designers Robin Johnston and M. Veronica Velasco made the gray type dance.

I am deeply grateful to this book's editor, Amy Cherry, whose sharp eye turned an essay series into a book and whose unbridled enthusiasm has made that process a delight. My agent, Mickey Choate, and his associates, Carolyn Larson and Robert Lescher, at Lescher & Lescher Ltd., in New York, provided wise counsel and unceasing encouragement.

My wife, Janine Steel, shaped this collection from word one, providing judgment, imagination, and patience when they were needed most. My mother, Suzanne Pederson, offered the unblinking criticism and unconditional support I've long taken for granted.

Finally, I want to thank each of the writers who contributed to this series. They worked hard on these essays, which are truly labors of love. This book is their book—and now it's yours.

PERMISSIONS